LIFE AFTER DENTISTRY

Retirement Lifestyle Readiness

SecondCareer

Retirement Program

Second Career Program
Copyright © 2024, 2006 by Alan Roadburg, PhD

Roadburg, Alan

Life After Dentistry

ISBN 978-0-9811740-9-9

1. Retirement - Lifestyle, non-financial. 2. Dentistry. 3. Self-help
I. Title

ABOUT THE AUTHOR

Dr. Alan Roadburg is an expert in retirement lifestyle planning with a diverse background in academia and practical application. He holds a PhD. in Sociology from the University of Edinburgh, and began his professional journey as a tenured professor at Dalhousie University. During his time there, he focused on Social Gerontology, the Sociology of Retirement, the Sociology of Work and Leisure, and Social Psychology. He also served as an Adjunct Professor at Simon Fraser University.

Dr. Roadburg made a significant career shift, establishing the Second Career Retirement Program. This transition allowed him to develop and present his unique Life Goal Planning approach to retirement, combining his academic knowledge with practical applications. Dr. Roadburg's work is grounded in extensive research. He interviewed 400 retirees, leading to the publication of his book "Work and Leisure in Retirement." More recently, he surveyed 2,400 retirees including physicians, dentists, teachers and Police Officers in the US and Canada, forming the basis for his series of books.

Alan's unique approach to retirement planning focuses on replacing the non-monetary satisfactions lost from work, aiming to create what he calls "The Perfect Retirement." His expertise and innovative methods have made him a valuable resource for individuals and professionals in retirement planning.

His books include: *The Perfect Retirement, Life After Medicine, Life After Dentistry, Life After Teaching, Life After Policing, What Are You Doing After Work?*, and *Aging: Retirement, Leisure and Work.*

ACKNOWLEDGMENTS

I want to express my gratitude to the many individuals who directly and indirectly contributed to making this book a reality. I am thankful to the thousands of people who participated in my retirement planning workshops over the years. Their involvement and feedback allowed me to develop, test, and enhance a Life Goal Planning approach to retirement planning.

A special thank you is extended to the retired dentists who took part in the research that is incorporated throughout this book. They are the true experts on 'life after dentistry' and their advice and experiences are a welcome addition.

Finally, I want to thank the Association of Retiring Dentists and Dr. Neil Hiltunen who became a major part of this project right from the very beginning. His input during the design and implementation of the questionnaire, as well as the final edit of this book, was invaluable.

If situations are defined as real,
they are real in their consequences.
(W.I. Thomas, 1923)

CONTENTS

LIFE GOAL PLANNING WORKSHOP

*The dash in re-tirement is intentional

LIFE AFTER DENTISTRY

INTRODUCTION

Because there are two forms of spending in retirement - time and money – it is necessary to consider two forms of planning for retirement - lifestyle and financial planning. These distinct planning procedures complement and enhance one another, but at the same time, they are worlds apart. To start with how they differ, financial planning is based on an established body of knowledge, and most financial advisers are highly trained accredited professionals. Unfortunately, things are quite different in terms of non-financial or lifestyle planning. Lifestyle planning involves identifying how you want to spend the rest of your life after you retire; anyone can claim to be an expert in this area. There are no formal training requirements or accreditation standards, and it is common to see books and websites in this area written by people with a vast array of backgrounds and experience, including financial planners, career planners, social workers, medical professionals, and retirees who suddenly become experts in retirement lifestyle planning.

THE TRADITIONAL APPROACH

The history of retirement lifestyle planning reveals why these problems occur. Being a relatively new field that emerged in the 1950s and motivated by a concern for employee welfare following retirement, a handful of corporations called on healthcare professionals to develop programs to help employees through the transition at the end of their careers. Retirement was viewed simply as giving up work, and the solutions related more to the symptoms than the cause of any problems. Because healthcare professionals created the early programs, the traditional approach tended to address health and aging issues rather than retirement. So, issues such as health, safety, nutrition, recreation, stress management, hobbies, travel, sex and aging, prepaid funerals, and so on formed the basis of the traditional approach to retirement lifestyle planning.

As a body of knowledge, retirement lifestyle planning is not grounded in solid research or theory. It is full of generalizations and value judgments and usually proposes a 'one-size-fits-all' or 'cookie-cutter' solution. Most retirement lifestyle planning authors today add their spin and recycle this original outdated approach because it has always been done that way. So why reinvent the wheel? The answer is simple. The wheel is broken. The Boomers are about to retire. They are the architects of a new retirement as they recreate retirement in their image, and the traditional approach does not adequately address their main concerns.

A NEW APPROACH

I am not a financial planner, and my interest in retirement planning evolved from an earlier interest in the Sociology of Occupations and Professions. During my PhD graduate work in Scotland at the University of Edinburgh, I was interested in the Sociology of Work and Leisure. I carried out research on this topic by focusing on a single activity that some people pursued as work and that others pursued as leisure. My fieldwork involved participant observation research among professional and amateur soccer players (football in Scotland) to discern differences in the work and leisure experience surrounding the same activity. I spent four months participating in the day-to-day training and social activities of a professional soccer club (Heart of Midlothian Football Club) and two amateur teams. This was supplemented with in-depth personal interviews among professional and amateur gardeners.

When I obtained a university teaching position, I wanted to extend my interest in the meanings of work and leisure to focus on people who were not working. I chose retirees. This research involved in-depth interviews with 352 retirees looking at work, leisure, friendships and life satisfaction. I gathered a great deal of data and information on these issues, and the results were published in my book, Aging: Retirement, Leisure and Work.[1]

Several main findings emerged from my early research experiences. First, regarding perceptions of work and leisure, when people are working, they tend to view leisure as time off work or free time. However, when they retire, because most of their time is free time, they tend to view leisure as pleasurable or enjoyable activities. So, retirement is not leisure. Second, when asked what they missed about work, the three most frequently mentioned items were social contact, having something to do, and daily routine. Interestingly, money was only mentioned by 9% of the males and 2% of the females as something they missed from work. This is not to suggest that money isn't important; far from it. However, this suggests that when people retire, they adapt to their financial situation, and if they identify areas that can be improved upon, they focus on the non-financial domain. Finally, the finding that had the most significant influence on my work in this area was that if people have problems in retirement, they most likely stem from boredom.

After six years of university teaching and research, I changed careers to concentrate full-time on conducting retirement lifestyle planning workshops. Following my research experiences, my initial challenge was to develop a program to help people replace satisfactions like social contact, having something to do, and a daily routine no longer provided by work. Having rejected the traditional model as ineffective and working with insights from the career change literature, I created a new approach called

Life Goal Planning. My career change from the University to conducting retirement lifestyle workshops for corporate clients occurred 30 years ago. Life Goal Planning has repeatedly been tested, refined, and improved.

This book bridges the gap between theory and practice. It originated in academic research and theory (my own and others). It developed and was perfected through hands-on and practical experience with thousands of pre- and post-retirees who attended and provided feedback on my workshops over the years. The result is not another spin on the traditional approach but a new paradigm or frame of reference in retirement lifestyle preparation.

Retirement today is not what it used to be. It is changing to reflect the emergence of a new breed of retirees, the Baby Boomers. The Boomers will live longer, retire richer, are more highly educated, and expect more from life in retirement compared to any group of retirees in the past. The main objective or purpose of this book is to provide you with the tools and insights to ensure that your retirement will be worthwhile and enjoyable. These tools do not focus on the financial domain and will not help you increase your nest egg or reduce taxes. Most people equate retirement planning with financial planning, but as this book will clarify, financial planning is a necessary but insufficient condition for retirement happiness. I would argue that financial planning is not retirement planning. It is money management. And because you will be spending time and money in retirement, you must manage and integrate both elements. If it is not obvious, the secret to retirement happiness lies beyond the financial realm.

Of course, money is essential, but during my work with retirees, I have met many people who are well off financially but do not enjoy retirement. I have met people who are just getting by financially but consider retirement the best years of their lives. This fact points to one undeniable conclusion: money alone will not guarantee retirement happiness. Unfortunately, most people do not think about planning for the non-financial side of retirement because they think things will look after themselves. Or, if they look for help, the standard or traditional approach to retirement lifestyle planning does not adequately prepare people to answer the most important question: How do you plan to spend your time for the rest of your life?

MAIN PURPOSE

This book serves three objectives: a) to guide your decision to retire, b) to provide insight and a process to ensure your retirement will be worthwhile and enjoyable, and c) to incorporate Life Goal Planning within your financial plan. Another element that distinguishes this book is that I avoid value judgments and generalizations. My goal is not to suggest or tell you what to do but to provide the tools to identify and create a retirement that you will consider enjoyable, worthwhile and purposeful. Creating a retirement that will be worthwhile and enjoyable is probably not going to appear magically. But if you are prepared to expand your horizons, use your imagination, think creatively, and do a little work, you will reach this goal.

YOUR RETIREMENT MENTORS

Retirement is a unique experience that means different things to different people. The problem is that most retirement lifestyle authors tend to ignore this fact by presenting what they feel are the necessary ingredients for retirement happiness based on the author's own retirement experience or a few case studies. Underlying this somewhat narrow perspective is an outdated notion of retirement based mainly on health professionals' earlier work in this field, where the emphasis was on what I refer to as the "what to look out for" approach.

To overcome these biases, I went to the experts. After all, who would know better about retiring than a large sample of retirees? I created the Life After Work online survey and received 2,400 replies from retirees in the United States (37%) and Canada (63%). The sample included Physicians, Dentists, Teachers, and Police Officers. This represents a broad spectrum of financially secure retirees.

YOUR RETIREMENT MENTORS

N = 635

Gender
Male.......91%
Female.....9%

Current Age
<58............4%
58-64 ......23%
65-71 ......51%
72+..........21%

Marital Status
Married 85%
Widowed 2%
Never Married 3%
Separated/Divorced 6%
Common law/Partnered.....4%

Health Status
Excellent 42%
Very Good 38%
Good................. 18%
Poor 2%

Age at Retirement
Under 58 ....14%
58-64 ....38%
65-71 ....40%
72 and over.....8%

Length of Retirement
0-5 years........71%
6-10 years......17%
11+ years 12%

Participation in Dentistry
Totally retired 49%
Work 1-2 days a week 24%
Work 3-4 days a week 27%

Type of Practice
General...........................84%
Specialty 14%
Solo................................. 1%
Group.............................. 2%

Retiring from dentistry can involve different considerations compared to retiring from other lines of work. To overcome these biases, I went to the experts. After all, who would know better about retiring from dentistry than dentists who are retired? I created the Life After Dentistry Online Survey and received 635 responses from retired dentists in the United States (54%) and Canada (46%). The subjects were located through The Association of Retiring Dentists (ARD), and the ADA in the United States, and the CDA in Canada. I refer to the research subjects as 'retirement mentors'. A mentor is a trusted counselor or teacher, and your retirement mentors include dentists with retirement experience. I was on the lookout for any differences between the U.S. And Canadian respondents and for the most part their replies were almost identical.

You will notice that 51% of the respondents did not classify themselves as fully retired. This is because it is relatively easy for dentists to in a sense ease into retirement by working fewer days a week, either continuing with their current practice, teaching, or other dental related activities. For example.

> *About two hours every two weeks every 2 to 3 weeks on friends who request to be seen as new patients.*
>
> *I am totally retired from practice, but I teach part-time at the Faculty of Dentistry 1/2 day a week for 10 weeks in the whole year.*
>
> *I volunteer one day a week in a clinic.*
>
> *I work as a dentist 2 to 3 days per week. However I take a week off for travel almost every 6 to 8 weeks.*
>
> *License is still active, I do humanitarian missions once a year.*
>
> *Totally retired, but am clinical instructor two half days a week.*
>
> *Work 4 to 5 days a week but at decreasing hours.*
>
> *Work as a consultant with an insurance company.*

You will also notice that only 9% of our respondents were women. This reflects the fact that traditionally dentistry has been a male dominated profession. According to the ADA Health Policy Institute, in 1978, only 15.9 percent of first-year dental students were women. In 2014, it was 47.7 percent. (ADA News, Women in dentistry see progress, continued challenges, January 18, 2016). Presumably if we were to conduct this research in the future we would have a far greater percentage of retired women dentists respond to the survey.

LIFE AFTER WORK SURVEY

The survey questionnaire (reproduced at the end of the book) included closed and open-ended questions and covered the main issues affecting retirement happiness. These included the decision to retire, type and degree of retirement planning, working in retirement, volunteer activities, moving after retirement, friendships, spousal relations, and overall satisfaction in retirement. The respondents were also allowed to express their opinions freely on the main attractions and drawbacks of retirement, and they were asked what advice they would give to others contemplating retirement.

Closed-ended questions provide possible answers. Sometimes, they can only choose one, for example, gender or age at retirement. In other cases, they can choose as many as they like, such as reasons for retiring. In this case, the totals will often exceed 100%, as most chose multiple replies. Open-ended questions, such as those about advantages, drawbacks, and advice on retirement, resulted in qualitative responses where the subjects were free to express their feelings through written responses. To give structure or order to the open-ended responses, each response was evaluated, and we identified general categories based on the type of response. This process enabled us to determine the percentages of respondents in each category.

The survey results are presented through bar graphs as a percentage of respondents. This could be based on all respondents or a sub-group. For example, their gender or age is based on all respondents. However, the question of why they chose to work in retirement is based on those who worked in retirement. We also applied cross-tabulations to analyze and compare one variable to another—for example, gender differences among those who chose to work or attitudes toward retirement based on health. The results often include a sample of qualitative direct quotes.

This type of research can have its limitations. Those people who feel strongly for or against retirement may be more likely to take the time to respond or respond in a particular manner. In addition, because the research took place online, some people could have been excluded.

Nevertheless, we were pleased with the response rate and the range of responses, and I believe our sample accurately reflects the experiences and opinions of most retirees. The research results are woven into the following information, and to my knowledge, The Perfect Retirement is the only lifestyle planning program that includes input from such a large group of retirees.

Most of the issues included are relevant regardless of economic conditions. Because the respondents shared their experiences and advice for your benefit, this unique resource can be extremely valuable for your future retirement, and you would be wise to learn from their experiences. I advise you to view their experiences and comments with an open mind and consider them based on your situation and needs.

LINK WITH FINANCIAL PLANNING

Early in my career, I realized that Life Goal Planning has an additional and very important benefit for retirement. It can provide an integral element often missing from a financial plan. Typically, when I present my workshop, I do so with a financial planner, and in most–if not all–cases, the planner stresses the importance of establishing a financial goal. In fact, according to the Financial Planning Association, "The financial planning profession exists to help people reach their financial goals and dreams".[2] The problem is that establishing a financial goal or dream is based on knowing how you want to spend your time in retirement, and based on my 20-plus years of workshop experience, I would estimate that only about one-third of pre-retirees have a solid retirement plan. Because Life Goal Planning can help you create worthwhile and enjoyable retirement plans, it can provide the missing element in personalizing your financial plan.

PLAN OF THE BOOK

There is an old saying, 'You can't control the winds, but you can adjust your sails.' Life Goal Planning will help you identify areas you can control or adjust in the non-financial domain and introduce you to various strategies to ensure your retirement will be worthwhile and enjoyable. It will give you an overall objective view of your future retirement plans or options in the context of your financial situation to enable you to make a rational decision about your best plan of action. Of course, money is important, but there are things you can do and possible solutions found by looking beyond the financial realm.

This book is not about saving money during a financial crisis or positioning your portfolio for a rebound. Nevertheless, if you are looking for a process that can point you in the right direction and get you started on the right road, Life Goal Planning, tested by thousands of pre and post-retirees over the past 30 years, can be your solution. Life Goal Planning can offer some unexpected benefits even if you decide to postpone your retirement. If you find yourself out of work and on the brink of retiring, if you don't have any options, it can provide some hope, guidance, and inspiration.

In a sense, this book does not have a definite ending. It ends when you find activities in retirement that you consider worthwhile and enjoyable, and this will happen at different times for different people. The first part includes various concepts and issues presented through a collage of conversations. The purpose is to bring your image of retirement in line with reality, make you aware of it, and provide insights into the key issues that can affect retirement happiness. Although the characters you will meet are fictional, don't let the conversational style fool you. The issues, theories, ideas, concepts, and examples we discuss are based on the real-life experiences of various participants in my retirement workshops. We begin with an overview of several important concepts used throughout the book. I argue that the standard view of retirement is outdated, negative, and could be a counterproductive, self-fulfilling prophecy. I present a new paradigm or frame of reference for retirement more compatible with the new breed of retirees. You will also learn the secret to retirement happiness.

The book includes two types of information: general text presented in a conversational format and additional or background information. The additional information includes the pertinent results from our research among retirees and is highlighted with a light gray background.

Chapter One (Fixing a Hole) introduces a new way of looking at retirement, including a full explanation of 're-tire with a dash'. I use this opportunity to 'fix' or 'repair' the sometimes unknown, false image surrounding retirement. This chapter outlines what retirement is or can be today rather than what it was in the past. The Baby Boomers will face a new retirement requiring a new perspective and guidelines.

Chapter Two (Do You Want to Know a Secret?) reveals the secret to retirement happiness based on how you will spend your time in retirement. It also includes a process to incorporate lifestyle and financial planning.

Chapter Three (Ticket to Ride) is an overview of a unique process to guide your retirement career so that it will be worthwhile and enjoyable. This process is outlined in detail in Part 2 through a series of do-it-yourself exercises. You will learn how to evaluate your retirement plans and maybe make them better, as well as how to come up with new ideas if needed. We also address the issue of what happens if you know what you want to do in retirement but, for some reason, you can't do it. You will learn that you have an 'ace up your sleeve'.

Chapter Four (A Hard Day's Night) examines working after retirement. I present several issues to think about, including the question, "Are you taking the easy way out?"

Chapter Five (Money Can't Buy Me Love) outlines the relationship between Life Goals and Financial Planning. Both planning methods complement and work in parallel, with changes in one influencing changes in the other.

Chapter Six (Did You Ever Have to Make Up Your Mind?) provides help with the decision to retire. Money is not the only consideration; you will learn a few techniques to turn an otherwise subjective decision into an objective one.

Chapter Seven (When I'm Sixty-Four) is in response to a question raised by The Beatles over 40 years ago. I present an entirely different way of looking at aging and argue that it has nothing to do with retirement.

Chapter Eight (With A Little Help from My Friends) focuses on how retirement can affect a marriage relationship and friendships. It includes real-life examples of emerging problems and how to deal with them. Of course, not everyone is married at retirement, so retaining and building new friendships can become even more important.

Chapter Nine (Our House) focuses on moving after retirement. We look at some potential problems and how to overcome them. What happens if one person wants to move but the spouse doesn't? Or, what happens if you move and later realize you made a mistake?

Part 2 includes the Life Goal Planning Workshop, the defining element of this book, designed to help you find a life after work that will be worthwhile and enjoyable. This is a self-help version of the workshop I have delivered to clients for over 30 years. It is not presented as a magic one-size-fits-all solution because each person's solution to finding a future lifestyle that will be worthwhile and enjoyable will be different. You will learn how to identify your Life Goal, evaluate your retirement plans, maybe improve them, and develop new activities and interests should you need them. You will also learn how to integrate your Life Goal with your financial plan and, ultimately, how to guide your retirement career.

The Life Goal Planning Workshop is not designed as armchair or bedtime reading. It is a hands-on workshop you can complete independently or with a small group. To understand and appreciate the value of Life Goal Planning, you must learn the process by completing the exercises. The process is presented in a generic mode, and it is up to you to develop and implement your plan. You will probably have to make a few adjustments across several retirement variables, and to see some results, you will have to put in the effort, keep your mind open to new insights and ideas, and think, brainstorm, and experiment. You can look for input from your friends, family, and perhaps a financial adviser, and it may take time.

You may notice that some topics that often appear in other retirement planning books are excluded from this book - for example, health tips, end-of-life resources, social services, retirement communities, or love and sex (sorry). Granted, these can be important, but they have nothing to do with the transition from work to retirement. Also, some topics included are dealt with from a slightly different perspective than you may expect. For instance, we look at working in retirement, and you are presented with the question: Are you taking the easy way out? As another example, I argue that aging has nothing to do with retirement. Although you will find this subject in most other books on retirement lifestyle planning, my approach and the way I develop it are quite different. Realizing that friendship is an essential element, your retirement mentors have a lot to say on this matter. They also have some excellent suggestions if you consider moving after retirement. The issues, theories, ideas, concepts, and examples presented in the following pages are grounded in the real-life experiences of various participants from my retirement workshops and the Life After Work Survey results.

TEST YOUR RETIREMENT LIFESTYLE READINESS

Before you begin, I encourage you to complete the Retirement Lifestyle Readiness Quiz starting on page W-2 in your worksheets at the back of the book. After you complete the Program, you can reevaluate your lifestyle readiness to see how it has improved.

Chapter 1

Fixing a Hole
(The Beatles, 1967)

A New Frame of Reference

I am a handyman. I have not received training in this area and don't have elaborate or expensive tools. However, I enjoy doing odd jobs around the house. When a section of my fence blew down during the winter, I fixed it temporarily. It needed a more permanent repair as well as a fresh coat of paint. I picked up the necessary supplies to complete the job. The weather was no longer an excuse; it was sunny and hot, and I was outside fixing the fence when my neighbor Dave poked his head over the fence.

"Hi neighbor," he said. "What's up? Do you need any help?"

"No thanks," I replied. "I can finish this on my own. It's not a big job. After I fix this post, I will paint the fence."

"Well, then I'll help you paint," he said with a smile.

I could tell that Dave had something on his mind. His offer to help me paint my side of the fence confirmed that things were somewhat out of the ordinary. Dave and his wife Diane had been good neighbors over the years. We didn't see each other socially, but Dave and I often chatted as we worked in our yards and had a good arrangement of lending each other tools. It was not usual for Dave to make such a generous offer, but I accepted his offer and told him I would be ready to paint in about an hour.

"OK," he said. "I'll just go in to change and join you later." He headed for his house. True to his word, Dave appeared with a paintbrush, a stool to sit on, and dressed in his working clothes. He was serious about helping me with the fence. I couldn't help thinking about how Tom Sawyer had convinced his friend to paint Aunt Polly's fence.

We worked quietly for a few minutes, and then he said, "I have been wondering. I know you work with retirees, and we have a bit of a problem. Diane suggested I talk to you. She said maybe you could help."

I had a good idea of what was on his mind. He was a teacher, and Diane was a pharmaceutical sales rep. A while ago, he mentioned that he was starting to think about retiring, and ever since he has kept making little remarks such as "Pretty soon, I will be free as a bird." I had the feeling, however, that he was hiding his true concerns about retirement.

"What's the problem?" I asked.

"We talked about this before," he said, "but lately, I have been thinking about retiring. Last week, Diane and I attended a retirement seminar her school held. It was quite, how should I put this, an eye-opener."

"In what way?" I replied.

"Well, mostly it was good, but I can't help but feel sort of scared. I have been teaching for over thirty years and like my work. I don't know if scared is the right word, but I feel uncertain about the future. I don't have to retire now. The problem is, I don't know what to do."

"Do you remember my friend Les?" he asked.

"Not exactly," I replied.

"He retired about a year ago, and I think he has real problems. It's not a money problem; he seems OK in that department. When he first retired, he kept telling me how busy he was. However, after a while, it seems he ran out of things to do. In fact, he got quite depressed. I haven't seen him for a while, and the last thing I want is to be like him, with everyone feeling sorry for me."

To shift Dave's focus away from thinking about one bad example and to start thinking about retirement in general, I said, "I can understand your concern, Dave. After all, retiring can involve major changes in your life. The problem is we are trained and educated for most things in life, except retirement."

"That is so true," he replied. "I hoped the seminar would help, but it didn't. I'm still confused."

"Why don't you tell me about the seminar you and Diane attended," I suggested.

As Dave dipped his brush into the paint bucket, he said, "Well, parts of it were pretty good. They talked about a lot of things, but all in all, at least for me, it was a bit of a downer."

I cringed because the course he attended likely followed a traditional approach to retirement education that is common today and that I think is out of date.

TRADITIONAL APPROACH TO RETIREMENT PLANNING

What I call the traditional approach tends to present a false image of retirement based on a somewhat haphazard tradition. To be more specific, retirement lifestyle or non-financial planning is relatively new. It evolved from trial and error rather than basic, high-quality research. Motivated by a vague moral concern for employee welfare following retirement, a handful of major corporations began developing programs in the 1950s to help employees through the transition awaiting them at the end of their careers. People in the health professions developed the original approach to retirement education, and the subjects covered reflected this orientation. The problems are that this model or approach is not based on adequately formulated research, some of the issues confuse retirement with aging, many do not apply to everyone, and they often include generalizations and subtle moral judgments about what you should or should not do in retirement.

I have seen statements such as, "You should always wait at least a year following retirement before making any changes in where to live" or, "For a happy and healthy retirement, you should become involved in something completely different at least once a year," or "Do nothing for at least a year following retirement." Notwithstanding that, these generalizations contradict each other, whenever I come across personal opinions and judgments about what people should or should not do in retirement, I react negatively, and most important of all, they can't help Dave with his dilemma. That's why I cringed when Dave said the course he attended was a downer.

When I asked what the course covered, he replied, "Mostly, they talked about financial matters. As I said, it was good. They had a few speakers, and some of them, especially the financial guy, knew his stuff. Diane and I have a financial planner advising us for a long time, so we already knew most of what he talked about."

"Did they go through other issues besides money?" I asked.

"That was part of the problem," he replied. "They talked about retirement being the best time of your life. They referred to it as the golden years. They don't look too golden to me. Anyway, the guy said that we would have an extra gazillion hours to fill in retirement, and he gave a few examples of people who retired and what they were doing." Dave put down his brush and said, "I have the course description in the house. I can't remember all the details. Should I get it?"

"Sure," I replied. "I'm curious to see what they covered."

He returned with the course description, and I could see by the topics included that it followed the traditional approach I referred to above.

"Do you want my opinion of the course?" I asked.

"Why not," he said. "You're the expert."

I suppressed my feelings about the traditional model and said, "Looking only at the non-financial side, I have a problem with some of the contents."

"A problem?" he replied with a puzzled look.

"I am suggesting, Dave, that you probably have a false impression of what your retirement will or could be like, and I don't think this course helped matters."

"I guess so," he replied. "I keep getting mixed messages about what to expect."

I explained that there are two distinct areas of retirement planning covering financial and non-financial or lifestyle issues. The financial side is based on an established body of knowledge, which most financial planners are highly trained and accredited to handle. Unfortunately, things are different on the non-financial side. Anyone can claim to be an expert in this field, but the body of knowledge on the non-financial side is weak.

"I refer to this as the traditional model," I said, indicating the seminar outline. "It was developed over forty years ago when retirement and retirees were different from today, but the problem is, it no longer applies. Retirees today, people like you, are a different kettle of fish. Most books and courses, including the one you took, are variations of the traditional model. That's why I told you I had a problem with this course."

However, the proof is in the pudding. The course Dave attended did not help him with his concerns about retirement. In addition, based on my experience, Dave is not alone in this regard. Most people have these same concerns when thinking about life after work.

"OK," I said. "Let me describe what you can expect. I can assure you that it is quite different from this. However, before we start, the sun is starting to get to me. I have been out here for a while, and I'm going into the house to get a cold drink. Do you want anything?"

"Sure," said Dave. "Whatever you're having will be fine."

The lifestyle side of retirement education involves many dimensions and issues, and given Dave's anxiety, I realized that I had to start at the beginning. I suspected that, like many people, he didn't understand retirement and that his image was probably out of date. It was also apparent that the course he took reinforced this false image. When we resumed painting, I pointed out that the first thing he had to do was reevaluate and update his image of retirement.

"I don't think that's the problem," he replied. "I have a pretty good idea of what retirement is. My problem is that I'm unsure if I am ready for it."

Dave's problem ran deeper than he realized. It was not simply a matter of being unsure if he was ready for retirement. His problem stemmed partly from the meaning he attached to retirement and his subsequent action - or, in his case, lack of action - toward it.

DEFINITION OF THE SITUATION

To appreciate Dave's problem and the solution I presented, we can take a brief look at a theory identified as "Situational Analysis". Most social scientists base their thinking and research pursuits on established social theory. It provides a framework or vantage point for analysis. My academic interests focused on a group of social psychologists, with an affinity for the insights of W.I. Thomas. Writing in the 1920's, Thomas developed a concept called "the definition of the situation". For our purposes, he demonstrated that one capacity that differentiates man from animals is that the latter act primarily on instinct, while the former have the ability to examine and deliberate before acting. He referred to the act of examination and deliberation as a stage that preceded action. We pause, and consciously or subconsciously try to make sense of a situation and based on our interpretation or the meaning we attach to that situation (our definition of the situation), we act accordingly. Thomas succinctly presented this insight in a single sentence: "If people define situations as real, they are real in their consequences".[1]

In other words, people respond not only to the objective features of the situation but also, and often mainly, to the meaning the situation has for them. This explains why two people faced with the same situation might react differently. If one person sees a glass as half-full, while another sees the same glass as half-empty, we have two different definitions of the same situation (viewing a glass of water). Alternatively, if two people attend a movie, one enjoys it, and the other doesn't, we have different definitions of that situation and two potentially different ways of reacting. Suppose a movie critic saw the same movie, they would define it differently and likely approach and respond to it in an entirely different way. Looking upon retirement as a situation defined differently by different people, one would expect different meanings, reactions to, and ways to approach retirement.

Getting back to Dave's problem of mixed feelings and uncertainty about retirement, I think he had two problems. First, his definition of the situation (his pending retirement) did not reflect reality. He did not base it on personal experiences but on observing the experiences of other retirees, the media, images of retirement in the past, and hearsay. Unfortunately, the course he attended exacerbated his false image of retirement (that's why I told him that I was troubled by the course). His other problem was that he lacked the tools to help him transition from work to retirement. Because no one can experience retirement in advance, there is no reason to assume that one can transition without proper guidelines.

I planned to present a few facts that might help him redefine retirement to reflect reality more accurately. I also planned to teach him the tools I developed to help ensure that his retirement would be worthwhile and enjoyable. By clarifying his definition of his pending retirement and providing him with the tools for the transition to retirement, he would be on his way to solving his dilemma.

THE JACK STORY

To underscore how our definition of a situation can influence behavior, I recall a joke that I call the Jack Story. It's an old joke, but I think the message is clear.

A salesman was driving home from a successful sales trip, thinking about his loving wife and children who would greet him when he arrived just in time for dinner. Suddenly, BANG, he had a flat tire. His first impression was, "Now I'll be late for dinner." As he got out of his car, he thought to himself, "Why am I worrying? So I'll be a little late. I made good money this trip; I'll fix the tire and be on my way." When he opened his trunk, he discovered the jack was missing. Again, he thought, "There is no point in getting upset. I passed a gas station a while ago, it's a beautiful day, so I'll walk to the gas station, get a jack, and be on my way." After walking a few miles, he thought, "I am in the middle of nowhere; for sure the guy will charge me for the jack. Well, it can't be too much. Anyway, I had a very successful trip, so it doesn't matter." As he pondered his predicament, he started to worry - "I am at his mercy. He could charge me anything he wants. I don't have any other options; he can really take advantage of me." As he got closer to the gas station, he got madder and madder, expecting to be overcharged for the jack. Finally, he reached the gas station; the attendant approached with a smile and said, "Yes sir, can I help you?" The salesman was so angry, he yelled back...

After telling him the Jack Story, I said, "The point is, because he convinced himself that he would be overcharged for the jack, he got so angry that he no longer wanted it. To apply this to retirement, if a person's image of retirement is negative and expects it to be empty and meaningless, they might end up thinking, KEEP YOUR !?@}#* RETIREMENT! I DON'T WANT IT ANYWAY!" And if they think that way, their retirement may turn out that way."

"It's only negative because I am confused about what I should do," said Dave.

"I realize that," I said. "But to help overcome your confusion, you must first clarify your retirement image."

"If you insist," he said as though to humor me. "Start clarifying."

"First," I explained, "I have a confession to make."

He paused, placed his paintbrush on the edge of the can, sat on his stool and said, "Start confessing, my son."

I continued to paint and said, "I have been involved in retirement education for more than twenty years, and my confession is that I hate the word retirement."

I use overheads to highlight crucial points when conducting group seminars and workshops. I stood there with my paintbrush, wondering how to replicate an overhead slide. The solution was obvious. I dipped my paintbrush in the paint can and wrote on the fence.

"You hate it," he exclaimed. He picked up his brush and started to paint. Obviously, my confession wasn't as exciting as he had hoped.

"The problem," I said, "lies not with the word itself but with a history of bad press and the false and negative images the word can conjure up."

"What do you mean?" he asked.

To explain what I meant, I asked him a simple question. I asked him to define retirement.

He thought about this, painted a few strokes on my fence, and said, "Well, I suppose it means giving up your job, ending your career."

"Yes and no," I replied.

"What do you mean by that?" he asked.

"Well, on the one hand, your definition reflects most people's general image of retirement. Even the dictionary defines retirement as withdrawal from active working life. Nevertheless, I disagree with the definition. Think about it, Dave. A definition should describe an entity. Your definition refers to what you are giving up. It doesn't describe, explain, or give us any idea of what retirement is. It's like defining day as not night or leisure as not work. Besides, if you define retirement as giving up work, we have a problem with people who ease into retirement or return to work. Are they retired or not?"

"They are semi-retired," he replied.

"So they are half or partially retired?" I said somewhat facetiously. "My point is that defining retirement as giving up work is the traditional image that no longer applies. As we discussed, this image focused on what people gave up rather than what they gained."

"Do you have a better definition?" he asked.

"I think so," I replied. "But first, let me ask you another question. Besides giving up work, what other meanings do we apply to the 'R' word?"

The 'R' word?" he replied inquisitively.

"That's how I refer to the word 'retire' because of all the negative baggage it carries," I said.

To help him answer, I continued, "For instance, in baseball, when a batter strikes out, we say he retired the batter. Can you think of other ways we use the 'R' word?"

He thought about this and said, "I know, to go to sleep."

That's a good one," I said. "We also use retire to refer to retreat, withdraw, or take out of circulation. And we refer to a shy or modest person as retiring. Are you beginning to see the problem?"

"I never thought about it that way," he replied.

PROBLEMS WITH THE 'R' WORD

All these meanings point in one direction - withdrawal. Of course, there is nothing wrong with retiring a debt or going to sleep if you are tired. The problem is that the "R" word implicitly reflects advanced age and other negative uses when referring to giving up work, business or a career. It reflects an image of retirement that prevailed in the past. One or two generations ago, the image of retirement saw people leaving work at age 65. They received a gold watch, the lucky ones received a pension, most did not lead a particularly fulfilling or lengthy life in retirement, and most did not expect much from retirement. We only have to think of our grandparents or, in some cases, our parents to evoke an image of retirement that we hope will not apply to us. In the past, expressions such as over the hill (perpetuated by greeting card companies) and a little help from the media reinforced this negative image of retirement. The problem is that the implicit negative meanings hidden in the "R" word are inappropriate and out of step with the new retirement.

Today, we are on the verge of significant upheaval. The Baby Boomers born between 1946 and 1965 are on the threshold of retirement, and they face life circumstances that are significantly different from those faced by their counterparts in the past. They are richer, will live longer, are more highly educated, expect more from retirement, and account for 56 percent of the adult population. Given these differences, the negativity that accompanies the 'R' word is simply out of step with a new generation of Boomer retirees.

Finding a neutral term to replace the "R" word can be challenging. Marketing and advertising specialists are particularly perplexed by this problem. They realize the enormity of this market but must tread softly to avoid alienating its members. Admittedly, we are only dealing with a name. Nevertheless, the meaning behind a name can often have far-reaching effects.

"The problem with the 'R' word," I continued, "is that retirement has had its share of bad press in the past, and most people don't stop to think about how that can affect their view of retirement. If you think of retirement as giving up work, retreating, withdrawing, or going to sleep, and if you see a connection to growing old, you do not have much to look forward to. It can become a self-fulfilling prophecy.

"The good news, Dave, is just because these negative characteristics applied to retirement in the past, there is no reason to assume that they apply to retirement or retirees today."

"Take a look at your friends," I said. "These are future retirees. It should be obvious that they will not withdraw or follow the old pattern when they retire. Perhaps now you can understand why I hate the 'R' Word. It is simply out of step with reality."

"I never thought of it that way," he replied. "It's true. I remember greeting cards about retirement that joked about it being the end of the line. I don't know if they have these kinds of cards anymore."

"I don't think so," I said. "The card companies probably realized people weren't buying these negative cards anymore. But we are still left with the problem of the 'R' word, so I will show you how we can redefine retirement to be more compatible with retirement today."

A NEW FRAME OF REFERENCE

When I started conducting retirement education workshops, I recognized the problem with the 'R' word, and one of my first concerns was updating the image and definition of retirement. I wanted to come up with a new word that would be instantly recognizable and effective, delineating what retirement is, not what it isn't. The word had to reflect the positive nature of retirement, and it could not refer to age because age has nothing to do with retirement. So, words such as senior, mature, elderly, or golden age (that's why I cringed when Dave told me that the seminar leader referred to retirement as the golden years) were out of the question. Eventually, I came up with a replacement for the 'R' word.

"One positive thing about the 'R' word is that it is instantly recognizable. So, for its replacement, we start with the 'R' word and add a dash." I added the dash.

"What image comes to mind now?" I asked.

He smiled and said, "Getting new tires for your car."

"Exactly. The word re-tire with a dash suggests getting new tires or a new set of wheels. When was the last time you bought new tires?" I asked.

"Believe it or not," said Dave, "we visited our son a few weeks ago, and I bought new tires before we left."

"So, how did you feel after getting new tires?"

"Well, I suppose it felt good. The tires looked good, and I felt good about the safety factor."

"When you get a new set of wheels, you feel great; you can go anywhere - around town, across the country - feeling confident that the journey will be safe and comfortable. Let it rain, let it snow, I don't care, I have new tires on my car. Tire manufacturers love this image - it helps sell tires.

"Now transfer this image to your re-tirement," I explained. "To re-tire with a dash is like getting a new set of wheels for your life. It can involve rejuvenation; you can go anywhere and do anything, and it allows for new opportunities; you can please yourself.

"Adding a dash also refers to mixing in something different to improve the original, like adding a dash of salt or humor. This is precisely what re-tire with a dash involves. We are adding something different or spicing up an outdated image of retirement."

This new description characterizes what the new Boomer re-tirees hope to gain from re-tirement. It implies preparation for a journey, movement, action, rejuvenation, freedom, and a fresh new start. In contrast to 'retire' (without the dash), which implies withdrawal, retreat or going to sleep, 're-tire' means a new beginning.

"From now on, Dave, whenever you see or think of the 'R' word, spice it up and mentally add the dash. Think of getting a new set of wheels to embark on a new life journey. It can be anything you want, and the best time to begin this journey is to follow a work career. When the time comes for you to say, 'I am re-tired', say it with pride."

RE-TIRE WITH A DASH

For our purposes, to re-tire (with the dash) refers to preparing for a new life journey. When you re-tire you gain something (a new lease on life). When you retire (without the dash), you give up something (work, your turn at bat, life). The only positive use of the word retire is in reference to going to sleep and paying off a loan. Moreover, because re-tirement does not refer to giving up work, it is possible to re-tire to a new line of work.

NOTE: From this point on, re-tire refers to preparing for a fresh new journey, and the best time to begin this journey is following a work or business career. It also refers to the act of rejuvenating your life. Re-tiree and re-tired refer to the rejuvenated individual taking the journey, and re-tirement refers to the time the journey takes place. The word retirement (without the hyphen) will refer to the old traditional use of the term as applied to generations of retirees in the past. You will also see it used in direct quotes from your re-tirement mentors.

"I like this new way of looking at re-tirement," said Dave.

"Then I think you will like my definition," I replied as I painted the following words on the fence."

"Re-tire with a dash is defined as a career earned from and following work."

"The key here," I continued, "is to think of re-tirement as a career. I am not suggesting you will work in re-tirement, although many people do. I suggest that, like most work careers, your re-tirement career will develop and evolve. In addition, by emphasizing that you earned re-tirement, we acknowledge its worth as a reward following work. It is something to be proud of. You have earned it."

Viewed this way, we are accurately describing the new re-tirement. It is positive, dynamic, progressive, and does not refer to age. This new concept does not carry any excess or negative baggage. Because it does not refer to giving up work, this eliminates the need for awkward phrases like 'semi-retired' when a re-tiree returns to work."

LIFE CAREER

I explained how a re-tirement career emerges as the fusion of the individual's work and leisure career. To start, I painted a line on my fence to represent a work career and said, "Imagine that this line represents all the jobs that most people hold during their work career. I realize that teaching usually follows a distinct career path, but most people start their first job, which leads to something else, which leads to something else, and so on. Moreover, when they reach the end of their work career, they often end up doing something that may be completely different from when they started their work career.

"The same is likely to happen with your re-tirement career," I replied. "It will develop and evolve, and what you end up doing may be quite different from what you have in mind now."

"I hope so," he replied, "because I have nothing in mind now."

RE-TIREMENT AS A CAREER

Re-tirement as a career is an important characteristic of the new re-tirement. Retirement without the dash suggested an implicit emphasis on retreat and referred to an event, the day after the last day of work, or as a life stage. The new re-tirement is more dynamic. It is a career that will develop and progress over time.

There are significant differences between a work and re-tirement career. The need for income and security guides most work careers, while the desire to enjoy oneself will guide a re-tirement career. I am not suggesting that job satisfaction does not influence a working career. However, let's face it, the bottom line is to earn a living and feel secure. If the opportunity to make more money or increase job security came along, most people would probably make the career move. Another difference between a work career and a re-tirement career relates to how much control a person has over how each will progress.

Most people fall into their first job based on various circumstances, like working there in the summer. For others, perhaps a friend or relative worked there, it may have been the first job offered, it paid more, or a Personnel Director decided to hire you. Having started that first job, your life took a specific direction. If you change jobs, it is likely that circumstance also partially influences the new job. If you look back on your work career, you can see how many small circumstances, along with the decisions of others, have influenced where you are now. Suppose your first job was with a different company. Your life may have turned out to be quite different. Circumstances and the decisions of others exert a strong influence on the development of a working career.

"The main benefit of your re-tirement career, Dave, is that you are the boss. You can take charge and guide your life so that it will be worthwhile and enjoyable. There will be uncertainties, but they will be minimal. The beauty of re-tirement is that if you ever feel something is missing or are not enjoying life to the fullest, you can make adjustments. Most people do not have this freedom in their working career."

"That's certainly true," he said. "But sometimes having all that freedom, or free time, can be a problem."

"Absolutely," I replied. "And that is what Life Goal Planning is all about. But let's take this one step at a time."

Next, I introduced Dave to another career represented by a line parallel to the work career line and said, "If you think about it, your leisure can also be viewed as a career. Like your work career, it has and will continue to develop and evolve. However, a major characteristic of your leisure career is that your work career highly influences it. As circumstances change in your work career, you may see parallel changes in your leisure career. An obvious example is if somebody is promoted to a more senior position and makes more money, their leisure choices may likely reflect this difference. On the other hand, we may choose some activities to compensate for our work or others as an extension of our work, such as playing golf with a client or friends from work. And sometimes there will be no relationship between the two."

To complete the image of a Life Career, I included the re-tirement career.

"Your re-tirement career is an extension of your work and leisure careers. Together they comprise your Life Career. Your re-tirement career will develop and evolve as the fusion of your work and leisure careers. It is the best of both."

"Re-tirement is the opportunity to do something worthwhile as with work, with the pleasure of enjoyment as in leisure. You no longer have to do what others expect of you, but what you freely undertake on your own. Job and family responsibilities are behind you, and you can draw on a wealth of experiences, insights, and realistic aspirations. It is a new career based on combining or amalgamating your previous work and leisure careers. In some cases, especially for women who traditionally live longer than men, a re-tirement career can be longer than a work career."

"It all sounds perfect," said Dave. "But I still have no idea what to do when I re-tire."

"That's understandable," I replied, "especially since the seminar you took gave you the wrong impression of what re-tirement is all about."

The sun continued to beat down, and Dave offered to get us another drink. He was gone for a long time, and I initially thought he had enough painting for one day. However, when he returned, he brought sandwiches. It seemed that his definition of his re-tirement situation was beginning to change, and he was willing to learn more. It also seemed that he was willing to continue painting my fence. Tom Sawyer would have been proud of me.

LIFE GOAL PLANNING

We ate in the shade, and it was clear that Dave could use more help than possible through our backyard chat. I told him that after working with pre-re-tirees for many years, I developed a process I called Life Goal Planning designed for people in his situation. Once he understood how it worked, he would have the tools to create a re-tirement that would be worthwhile and enjoyable. I indicated we didn't have time today to go through the process, and painting my fence wasn't the ideal learning environment. I suggested that we could meet again to go through the process but that we could cover some other areas to give him greater insight or clues into the new re-tirement with a dash. He liked the idea of meeting again, and I enjoyed having him continue to paint my fence.

When we resumed painting, I said, "You have to remember, Dave, there are two forms of spending in re-tirement. You will be spending time and money, and the problem is, when most people prepare for re-tirement, they think mainly about the money side - financial planning. Of course, money is very important, but don't underestimate the significance of how you spend your time in re-tirement."

"But the two are related," said Dave. "It costs money to spend time, you know what I mean."

"I know exactly what you mean," I replied. "I agree that they are related. I am suggesting that because there are two forms of spending in re-tirement, there should be two forms of planning for re-tirement. Planning how you will spend your time should not left up to chance. Also, because financial planning is based on having a financial goal, which in turn is based on knowing how you will spend your time, the two forms of planning complement each other, and that is what Life Goal Planning is all about."

"Obviously, not everyone has this problem," I added. "I have met many people who can hardly wait to re-tire because they have a million things they want to do. But I have run hundreds of re-tirement workshops, and in my experience, close to seventy percent of pre-re-tirees do not have concrete plans for re-tirement."

"I know," said Dave. "That's what frustrates me. I know I have this great opportunity, but I don't want to jump into it yet. I just don't know what to do with myself when I re-tire."

RE-TIREMENT MENTORS' ADVICE

There are several reasons why Life Goal Planning can benefit you in re-tirement, but the main reason is when asked what advice they would give to other dentists who are contemplating re-tirement, the most frequently mentioned recommendation from your re-tirement mentors was to plan your time and remain active. This question cuts to the chase - it's the bottom line. They are speaking from experience and had the opportunity to summarize their feelings about re-tirement in a single statement. Their responses are summarized on Chart 1-1.

Chart 1-1. Advice from your Re-tirement Mentors

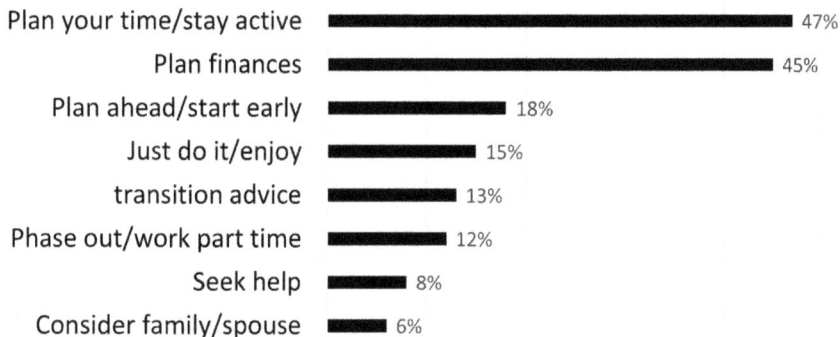

Advice	Percentage
Plan your time/stay active	47%
Plan finances	45%
Plan ahead/start early	18%
Just do it/enjoy	15%
transition advice	13%
Phase out/work part time	12%
Seek help	8%
Consider family/spouse	6%

PLAN YOUR TIME

It should not come as a surprise that the most frequently mentioned advice focused on planning how you will spend your time in re-tirement. This was an open-ended question so they could respond with anything. In some cases, the reference was very general, such as "Have some structured activity to go to, once you stop practicing dentistry", to specific recommendations such as, *"Develop hobbies and give back to society."* When you learn how to apply the Life Goal Planning techniques, you will be well on your way to having a plan.

As long as you are curious, have things you want to learn and do, you'll be just fine.

Be sure to have things that you REALLY enjoy doing outside dentistry. You need to have things that make you want to get out of bed early EVERY day.

I hope that you have a lot of other interests that you can fall back on to fill your days and give them meaning once your dental practice is gone. Financial security is only a part, albeit an important part, of the ability to have a meaningful and enjoyable retirement. An inquiring mind and a broad range of interests and activities is VERY important.

I would recommend that dentists plan for a future that would include something to give meaning and purpose to their time. Include in that plan something other than dentistry.

I've spoken with a number of dentists since I've retired, asking me for advice. I find most dentists seem like they want to retire earlier but have self imposed barriers preventing them from retiring. They are worried about what they will do with all of the extra time mainly. Loss of identity, money are other factors.

Make sure that you have a variety of interests that you want to pursue. You need to have some things to replace the stimulation of practicing dentistry.

Make sure you know what you will do with your time in retirement. If you do not have a clue how you will spend your days and you still like what you are doing, don't retire. If you have a high standard of living make sure you can cut that back and still be happy and have things to do.

One main point that everyone in any profession/job/career MUST know when considering retirement; "make sure that you have something to retire to". Tell that to everyone.

Plan ahead, start now doing hobbies that interest you and you can get more involved in during retirement. Set it up so you can do what you want when you want and don't sit around idle.

Planning or finding a purpose, activities and camaraderie prior to retiring is as important, if not more important, than financial planning.

Please find a new passion. I know, we as dentists, are very driven and passionate about our profession. If you don't find a substitute for that you will feel lost.

So many friends seem at loose ends once they retire because their work was their life. I have enough interests now that I wonder now how I had time to work and since my health is now deteriorating I am glad I retired early enough to do some of things I wanted to.

Spend some time thinking specifically about what you want to do when retired. Make a list and start some of these activities at least on a small scale before you retire. Otherwise inactivity takes over for a while and you may feel a greater loss from your former important, active role as a dentist to a less active civilian. It does tend to balance out after time but start new activities sooner rather then later.

The advice is different depending on what age one is retiring at. If one is retiring at age 65 to 70 the advice might be more along the lines of 'find a hobby' or 'start traveling. As for someone like me who decided to retire at age 61 my goal or mission was to find another purpose or passion.

Think of your life as a person not as a dentist. Dentistry gave you a life style but it should not define who you are. The sooner most Dentists realize that, the faster they make the transition to the rest (some may say, best) of their lives.

You must retire to something and not just from Dentistry. Not necessarily a new full time activity but at least something with a bit of order to it.

PLAN YOUR FINANCES

Forty-five percent encouraged you to plan your finances – the earlier the better. Although Life After Dentistry does not deal directly with financial planning, you will learn how Life Goal Planning can actually enhance your financial plan. Here are a few comments from your re-tirement mentors.

1) Owe no money to anyone. 2) Know what your monthly expenses are for housing, travel, entertainment, etc. 3) Determine if any of your children or aging parents are in need of financial assistance for whatever reasons, divorce, health, etc. 4) Have a good financial knowledge and don't depend entirely on someone else to manage your money.

Be prepared financially- put away more than you feel you really need because special circumstances, kids, and all that you want to do will take more of your finances than you might expect - doing this will give you a lot of comfort in retirement. You will be able to relax knowing you have enough money to see you through. Move slowly with your plans in the first year and give yourself that time to plan your next moves, be it travel, buying vacation properties, investments, etc. If you are financially prepared, all else follows easily.

Get out of debt as soon as you can and invest in your retirement as early as you can...Social Security is a poor investment with little return. Don't count on Social Security to be of much help when you retire.

I think if you have enough money to retire everything else seems to fall into place. Start saving from the first - don't wait till the end of your career or you probably won't be able to retire with confidence and less stress.

Investigate all the aspects of your post work financial life and for a year pre retirement try and live to that level while still working. Know your daily costs.

It's never too early to start serious planning. Learn to be the expert who oversees your advisers (nobody loves and understands you and your money like you do).

Plan financially to put 10% of your income away for retirement from the second year of working, no later than the fifth year.

Save from day one. Treat your savings as a bill that needs to be paid each and every month. Fully half of your retirement savings will come from what you save in your first 10 years in practice. Don't make any stupid investments, and don't invest in things you don't know. Do your homework so you know what your advisors are doing for (not to) you.

Start looking at the future immediately after starting practice, live an affordable lifestyle, look after needs as a priority and not wants. Don't borrow for 'toys'. Plan with your spouse what is their priority and be disciplined. Use expendable income for boats, expensive cars and skidoos.

PLAN AHEAD/START EARLY

Start saving from the first - don't wait till the end - of your career or you probably won't be able to retire with confidence and less stress.

Ensure adequate savings to enable retirement to a lifestyle of your choice. Plan ahead on activities which you will enjoy doing after retirement and pursue them.

Plan an exit strategy at least five years before - think about your family not just about yourself

It's never too early to start serious planning. Learn to be the expert who oversees your advisers(nobody loves and understands you and your money like you do)

Prepare at least 1 or 2 years ahead. Get your financial status in good standing way before considering retirement.
START PLANING NOW - NO MATER WHAT YOUR AGE.

JUST DO IT/ENJOY YOURSELF

Several people referred to what I call the 'Nike Approach' - just do it! Others offered more philosophical advice; encouraging you to enjoy yourself in re-tirement. For example:

Just do it. As you close one door another one opens!

Do it before health intervenes.

Do it soon, but stay involved. give back there is a lot of need out there

Do it when time is right and make sure you plan for it.

Do it with joy. Life is great but very short.

Do it!! But find something meaningful to do with your time and resources to benefit humanity, not just please yourself.

Go for it! Get out when you are still healthy!

If they feel ready to change course, pursue it.

Just do it when it's the right time. Only you can know the right time. You may screw up, but that's how it is.

Plan for it and enjoy it. Do not believe you must die at the chair.

Plan well, but if you have the means to do it, DO !! And enjoy the next part of your life.

TRANSITIONAL ADVICE

Some people gave specific advice referring to the transition to retirement. For example;

Consider an associate 2 or more years before you plan to retire.

Consider volunteer dentistry, continue CE credits to qualify for a volunteer licence.

Don't sell your practice too soon. Take as many breaks as you need to continue enjoying dentistry and earning a good income. Be prepared for episodes of major stress when selling your practice. Touch base and consult with a variety of trustworthy people. Don't just listen to good advice, have the resolve to implement it. No one can walk through that door for you. Ultimately you have to walk it alone.

Get a reliable, confident, quality associate to work for you for 3-4 years; who would then buy you out over time. As well, do a full makeover of the practice to make it saleable.

Gradually faze yourself out rather then cold turkey.

Hopefully you have lived a responsible lifestyle, saved for retirement and did not upset the cart with investments. If possible have a responsible dentist slowly take over your practice as you slowly reduce your own involvement. Make the time to allow yourself to enjoy your interests like travel. Postponing retirement reduces these opportunities. SEMI-RETIREMENT while still possible is definitely the best option.

I was able to find an associate who eventually bought the office and then hired me as an associate under the same contract. I was able to reduce my hours and take more vacation time for a period of three years.

Make sure you are financially secure. Have a transition plan in place so you can leave your patients in good hands when you are gone. Announce your retirement plans to your staff and patients at least six months before your retirement date so you and your patients have the opportunity to say 'Good-bye' to each other.

Make sure your transition of the practice is a good one. I sold to a corporate entity and that made it very easy and smooth. Plus I got more for my practice than the brokers were willing to do.

Really find an associate with the same values and try your hardest to make them successful. Then they will want you still to contribute and still be part of the practice. The staff will love the nice transition and you can work as much or little as you want.

Reduce your work days from full time to say 3 days per week so you start to have more leisure time to try out what you plan for retirement. Get an associate dentist into the practice to help them grow into the dentist you'll be happy to leave your patients in their care.

WORK PART-TIME

If you are in good health, work part time a bit longer than you had originally planned or thought about. But above all make sure you are well prepared financially. Living to 100 yrs is possible and it can tax your plans.

On my favorite coffee mug is a perfect saying: Do what you like, like what you do. I have been most fortunate to be able to remain active in dentistry. I still enjoy the profession. By cutting my hours, I have so far been able to keep away from burn out. At 57, I am cutting down my hours significantly giving me time to enjoy with family at home while keeping adequate income stream. At present, I would like to keep my nose in the office a few days a week till I am 68.

If you are in good health and still love dentistry and interacting with staff, and patients, you might consider working part time or volunteering at a free dental clinic.

DO NOT RETIRE TOO SOON!!! If you enjoy what you do - slow it down but DO NOT walk away cold. If you have good health and skills - continue to serve others.

OTHER ADVICE

Several people gave advice that did not fit into any of the above categories including maintaining your health, housing, and general reflections on life in re-tirement.

Eat well and exercise in the decades before retirement so your body is in good shape to enjoy its leisure time.

I found it hard to live in same community with past patients, always asking for dental advice and about treatment options.

Make sure that you are living in an area that you wish to live in for the rest of your life so that you don't have to move. For example, moving from a poor disadvantaged area of the country to a more sophisticated region can be very expensive, although with good investment savings and careful management, very much worthwhile and achievable.

Retire when you do not yet have to. It is a very good feeling to put up the drill when you are at the top of your game.

Take care of your health - nothing is as important as this - NOTHING. Get your financial world in order early. Taper off your commitments to the office gradually - -think about volunteering to the under served - you have a skill set that is in big time demand

Take the time to plan. Make sure your spouse/significant other is on board with your decision and understands the implications on his/her life as well as yours.

Too late now to change much. Try to get a good balance in the years you may have left. You will never have enough money, but your future is a lot shorter. Enjoy Every Day!

Value your health. There is nothing without it, retire before it begins to decline. Don't practice until your work begins to deteriorate. Be sure to have a plan and follow it through. Don't retire and just let life happen to you. Boredom is the wolf at the door! Stay mentally busy.

The message is clear. Money alone cannot guarantee re-tirement happiness. How you spend your time can be the most important element contributing to re-tirement happiness. To emphasize this point, I asked Dave if he knew anyone who was financially well off and not enjoying re-tirement.

"I sure do," he replied. "You've just described my brother-in-law. He retired a few years ago and was having some real problems. Money-wise, he was OK, but he used to be a high-powered executive, and my sister kept complaining about him hanging around the house all the time. Eventually, he settled down. However, he went through some rough times. I suppose my friend Les is in this situation, and if something doesn't happen soon, I will be in that situation."

"On the other hand," I said, "through my research and workshop experience, I have met people living below the poverty line who said that re-tirement was the best time of their life. Clearly, re-tirement happiness involves more than money. My program is called Life Goal Planning because re-tirement today, the new re-tirement, in many ways, involves uncharted territory. First, as I explained, the old traditional lifestyle planning approach is out of date. Therefore, we need a new set of directions for re-tirement happiness that focuses on how you will spend your time. Second, each person's re-tirement is unique. You can look at others, read about it, or attend seminars, but your experience will be unique. Just because your friend Les is having problems doesn't mean you will have problems. Because of this, you could use some guidance. The third reason is that you cannot truly understand what re-tirement will be like until you experience it. There are no dress rehearsals, so a proven method will help guide you."

"If I don't know what it will be like until I re-tire, how can you help me?" he asked.

"That's a good question," I replied. "But do me a favor, and let's return to this question. After you learn about Life Goal Planning, you can answer the question yourself."

"OK," he replied.

"As I said, re-tirement is unique because there are no dress rehearsals. When we experience other life changes, we usually have a good idea of what it will be like. When most people start working full-time, it is not a complete surprise. Why? Because we had some experience in this area by going to school. We learned about punctuality, competing with others, and so on before we started to work full-time. In addition, many people have part-time jobs in the summer, so they have a good idea of what working full-time would be like before they finish school. However, re-tirement is different. You can't experience it in advance.

NEW FOUND FREEDOM

Most people do not have much experience with extended periods of free time. When you were at school, you had summer vacation, and when you joined the world of work, you probably had a few weeks' holiday each year. Nevertheless, re-tirement is different. It's not like a vacation. Time can be your greatest ally or nemesis. The questions you must face include whether your gains will outweigh your losses. How are you going to use your new freedom? Will you use it to replace the satisfactions lost from work, to help you grow in a satisfying or fulfilling way, or will you rely on the vague hope that life will somehow take care of itself? Likely you could use a little help.

Before introducing Life Goal Planning, I wanted to clarify a few issues that many people associate with re-tirement but that, on a closer look, can inhibit re-tirement happiness. The first is the misplaced notion of confusing re-tirement with aging. I present this in more detail in Chapter 7.

"Dave, I recall when we talked about the retirement (without the dash) seminar you attended, the course included several subjects that related to health and aging, such as medicine, keeping fit, and safety at home. Did the speaker cover safety at home and medicine?"

"We didn't spend much time on this, but I recall that they did mention them."

"First of all, given that re-tirement is a career earned from and following work, what does safety at home or medicine have to do with re-tirement?"

Dave thought about this and replied, "If you put it that way, absolutely nothing."

"OK," I continued, "What does keeping fit, nutrition, and health have to do with re-tirement?"

"Everything," he replied. "If you're unhealthy, how can you enjoy your re-tirement?"

I could see I had my work cut out for me. This argument is common and underlies a misconception requiring clarification, so I applied some logic.

"I agree that health is important, but would you agree, Dave, that keeping fit, nutrition, and good health are important and could affect enjoyment while working?"

"Of course they could," he replied.

"What about when you were younger, like at school, were they important then?"

"Health is always important," said Dave.

"OK, so we agree. Health is always important, not just at re-tirement."

"For sure," he quickly responded.

"Have you ever attended a course on, say time management?"

"As a matter of fact, I have," he replied.

"Did you discuss keeping fit, health, or nutrition in this course?"

Dave looked at me as though I was crazy. "Of course not," he replied.

"Why not? Isn't health important for managing your time?" I fired back.

"I suppose so, but it's a separate issue."

"Well, if health is important at all stages in life, not just re-tirement, and if it is a separate issue for a work-related course, why should it be part of re-tirement planning? Remember, we are talking about changing from a work to a re-tirement career."

"Because we are getting older, and eventually, our health may become a problem," said Dave.

"So, it's not a health or a re-tirement issue, but an age concern," I replied.

"I guess so," he replied.

"So, we agree that a lecture on health does not belong in a course on re-tirement."

"If you put it that way, I guess not," he replied with a smile.

"How were health and fitness handled at the workshop? Did they bring in a speaker?"

"Yes, I think she was a nutritionist."

"Now be honest, Dave. After hearing her presentation, did you change your eating or exercise habits?"

A slight smile came to Dave's face, and he said, "Pass the beer and pretzels; I just ran out."

He didn't have to respond. People know what they should and should not eat or how much exercise they should do, and a speaker, no matter how well-intentioned, is not likely to change things - certainly not in the long run. I maintain that a speaker on health can be a detriment in a re-tirement education program.

I reminded him of two things we agreed on. First, that health is not a re-tirement issue, and second, he did not change his eating or exercise habits after the nutrition lecture. It follows, therefore, that the only thing the health lecture accomplished was to reinforce the false assumption that when people re-tire, they will likely be sick or get old. If not, why include it?

"The main problem," I said, "is if you believe there is a connection between re-tirement and poor health or old age, it could become a self-fulfilling prophecy. You could believe it to the point that you may create a problem. If you view retirement the old traditional way as withdrawal, putting out of commission, going to sleep, and so on, you can see why some retirement books or courses include a discussion on health. But if you view re-tirement as changing careers, health becomes a separate issue."

"I think I see what you are getting at," he said.

I pointed out that re-tirement is not a disease, and it never has, nor ever will, kill anyone. If a person is despondent, bored, lonely, or inactive, these can have a negative effect on health and longevity. I am not denying this fact. These conditions, however, are not exclusive to re-tirement. They can occur at any stage in life.

I continued, "The problem is, some writers and seminar leaders who discuss exercise or eating habits leave the impression that re-tirement can be bad for your health. Nothing could be further from the truth. As I see it, the only connection between re-tirement, health, and exercise is that you will no longer be able to use the classic 'I don't have enough time' excuse.

Re-tirement is the opportunity to plan your own time."

Once Dave realized that aging and health were not re-tirement issues, we were making significant progress in clarifying his definition of his re-tirement situation.

To identify another potential problem, I said, "I see they also covered retirement activities such as travel, leisure, hobbies, volunteering, and second careers. And here's an interesting topic: sex after 60. I suppose sex could be classified as a re-tirement activity."

"I hope so," said Dave.

"I hate to disappoint you," I said. "But sex is not a re-tirement activity."

"What?" he replied, acting surprised. "That does it. I've made up my mind. I'm never going to re-tire."

"Seriously, Dave," I said. "So, people have sex after 60. What does that have to do with re-tirement? Perhaps if they called it sex after giving up work, then it would at least sound relevant to retirement without the dash. By calling it sex after 60, they are referring to age, not to re-tirement. Like health and aging, sex is a separate issue that has nothing to do with the transition to your re-tirement career. You may have learned something in the workshop, but you must admit, sex is an inappropriate topic in a re-tirement course."

"If you insist," said Dave. "It may not be relevant, but it sure would spice up your workshop."

"I'll keep that in mind," I said. "And I'll call you in as an expert speaker."

Glancing at the course outline, I said, "I see the course included a section on managing stress. Clearly, the person who designed this course regards retirement as stressful. If that's the case, you would be wise never to re-tire. No wonder you have mixed feelings, Dave."

My favorite example of an irrelevant and inappropriate retirement topic is a discussion on funerals. I came across this issue in a book on retirement, and it is clear how the author views retirement and the type of negative message this sends to the reader.

Another issue that can create problems is the assumption that re-tirement is like leisure. Referring to the retirement course outline, I asked Dave how they presented this issue.

"I can't remember all the details," he answered. "But I remember him saying that retirement was like leisure earned from a lifetime of work. He also talked about taking a leisure interest and somehow working it into your re-tirement. I suppose that means I will be spending my re-tirement painting fences."

"If we don't finish soon, that may be the case," I agreed.

After refilling Dave's paint bucket, I said, "Actually, Dave, I wanted to talk about this because many people think about re-tirement as leisure, which is not necessarily the case. I agree that you earn re-tirement from work, but I do not agree that it is leisure. If you recall our discussion on life careers, I pointed out that your re-tirement career involved a fusion of your work and leisure careers."

To explain this distinction, I asked him to define leisure. He thought about it briefly and said, "I suppose it's doing something unstructured, outside work, doing something in your free time."

"That's a good definition," I replied. "And we use the term leisurely to do something without haste. So, my next question is, if leisure is free time or doing something slowly, would you say this is an accurate description of re-tirement?"

"Well, it's free time," he replied. "But I hope it won't be too leisurely."

"So, we agree. Our definition of leisure does not suit re-tirement. Besides, earlier you agreed that re-tirement was a career earned from and following work."

"Yes," he said.

"Another problem is that sometimes we think of leisure as secondary or trivial pursuits. However, re-tirement is a non-trivial pursuit. Clearly, they are not the same."

LEISURE AND RE-TIREMENT

When I taught at the university, I undertook a research project examining perceptions of work and leisure among re-tirees. When we asked whether they viewed re-tirement as leisure, in most cases, they did not view it that way. We found an interesting distinction between pre- and post-re-tires when asked how they defined work and leisure. Before people re-tire, they tend to look at leisure as free time (similar to Dave's definition). However, after they re-tire, because most of their time is free time, they differentiate between work and leisure activities based on degrees of enjoyment. They defined leisure as enjoyable activities and work as not-so-enjoyable activities. They also differentiate between work as other-directed and leisure as self-directed.

This brings us to a common problem among some re-tirees who think they can take a former leisure interest, increase the time spent on that interest, and that it will be as much fun or as meaningful during re-tirement. Travel is a good example here. While working, travel generally derives its meaning in contrast to our everyday life and work. The novelty and excitement of travel can soon wear off, however, if that is all there is to your life. This does not suggest that not all leisure interests will serve the same purpose in re-tirement or that travel will not be enjoyable when one re-tires. The point is that many leisure interests derive their meaning in contrast to work; if work is gone, the leisure interest can similarly lose its meaning. As stated earlier, re-tirement is a career that will develop and evolve as the fusion of your work and leisure careers. It is the best of both and the opportunity to do something worthwhile as with work, with the pleasure of enjoyment as in leisure.

It was time to give Dave a few more clues about what he could expect in re-tirement, so again, I turned to the fence.

Looking somewhat perplexed, he asked what it meant.

I explained that it stands for Central Life Focus. This concept initially applied to work, implying that work is a dominant sphere in our lives. The type of work we do and our level within the workplace exerts considerable influence on many other aspects of our lives. It can influence our thinking and lifestyle and demands a significant portion of our time and energy. For instance, our involvement in the workplace determines how much money we will have to spend, the goodies we can buy, the type of friends we will choose, our leisure interests, and how we will spend our time and money in re-tirement. It determines where we will live and may even influence whom we will choose as a spouse. As discussed earlier, our leisure career parallels our work career, and the latter influences the former.

"When you give up work," I said, "by default, re-tirement will become your Central Life Focus. I am not suggesting that you will have a problem replacing your CLF in re-tirement. All I am saying is that the difference between work and re-tirement as a CLF is that work generally involves one activity. In contrast, re-tirement may consist of several activities. Also, many lifestyle choices formed during your work and leisure careers will carry over to your re-tirement career. Again, I am generalizing, but often we get used to having a single CLF, and some people need a dominant CLF when re-tired. Others can quite happily spread their involvement over several activities."

"For some people, a leisure activity can become a Central Life Focus, but for most people, it is not enough to simply spend more time in a leisure activity. I am not suggesting that a leisure interest will not be enjoyable or serve the same purpose in re-tirement. I am simply pointing out that many leisure interests derive their meaning in contrast to work, and if work is gone, the leisure interest can similarly lose its meaning or is insufficient to replace a CLF."

"But I know somebody who contradicts what you are saying," said Dave. "I have a friend who loves to golf, and he could hardly wait to re-tire so he could spend all his time golfing. He repairs golf clubs in the winter and is a club marshal. He is involved in golf and seems quite happy in re-tirement."

"That's a good example," I replied. "But it doesn't contradict what I just said. It sounds as though he is not just spending more time playing golf. He expanded his interest through other golf-related activities. He started a small business repairing clubs, and presumably, as a marshal, he was involved in administrative activities. Together these activities constitute his CLF in re-tirement. I am willing to bet that if he did not expand into other activities and played more golf, his re-tirement would not be as fulfilling, and he would feel that something was missing from his life."

I asked Dave what he did for leisure, and he mentioned playing cards and camping. Using camping as an example, I asked him to explain why he enjoyed camping.

He replied with several reasons that characterized camping and added, "It's a good break from work."

To develop this thought further, I said, "Would it be correct to assume that part of the reason you enjoy camping is because it is completely different from your work? For example, it's outdoors, and work is indoors; work can be constricting, camping is freely chosen; work is highly structured, camping is the opposite; plus, as a bonus, you can camp with whoever you choose."

"Absolutely," replied Dave. "As I said, it is a break from work. Sometimes my job can get quite hectic, and camping is total relaxation.

I asked how camping might be different if he was re-tired.

He replied, "Well, we might go more often because I would have more time. On the other hand, we might go to different places. I suppose it might be a bit different now that you mention it. When Diane and I go camping, we enjoy getting away from it all. We may only go for a week or sometimes for a weekend, but I enjoy nothing more than driving into the country, especially when things are going crazy at work. Then again, I like my work, and after being away for a few days, I am anxious to get back to it. It's true, if I didn't have work to come back to, camping might not be the same."

"As you can see, your feelings about camping are tied somewhat to your feelings about work. In addition, it is enjoyable partly because it contrasts and is a break from work. At the same time, I wouldn't be surprised if you sometimes think about work when camping. So, it is reasonable to expect that your feelings about camping, or any leisure activity, may be somewhat different when you re-tire."

"Does that mean I will no longer enjoy camping when I re-tire?" asked Dave.

"Absolutely not," I replied. "It will still be enjoyable but may not serve the same function in re-tirement. It will take more than camping to replace the satisfaction lost from work. Your golfing friend is a good example of this."

"Another way to think about re-tirement," I continued, "is that it's like winning a mini lottery."

"Yeah, but I worked hard to pay for my re-tirement, whereas a lottery is pure luck."

"Absolutely", I replied. "Moreover, these are the same main concerns you must consider in planning for re-tirement. You have to ensure your money lasts and figure out how you will spend your time. Spending time is what Life Goal Planning is all about. Congratulations on your windfall."

"I haven't re-tired yet," said Dave.

"OK, congratulations on your pending windfall."

WINNING A (MINI) LOTTERY

As an interesting parallel, studies suggest that most lottery winners keep working because having a job is more than just about money. According to one study, money is important, but many benefits of work play a significant role: relationships, achievement needs that people have, and status needs outside of money[2].

We agreed that a break was in order, and as we cooled ourselves in the shade, Dave's wife, Diane, joined us. "You guys have been in the sun too long. How's it going?"

We'd had enough by this point, even though my fence was unfinished.

"I don't know about you," I said, "but I have had enough painting for today, and I have spent too much time in the sun. I want to continue our talk, so why not pick up where we left off next weekend?"

"I would like that," said Dave. "I'm still waiting to learn about Life Goal Planning."

"I would happily share it with you," I said.

"OK," said Dave, looking over at Diane. "We can meet at our house next weekend."

He paused momentarily and asked, "Would you mind if we called Les to see if he wants to join us? I think he could use it."

"By all means," I replied. "That would be a good idea. The process works best with a small group."

"Is Les married?" I asked.

"Yes," Diane replied. "I am quite friendly with his wife."

"Then ask her if she wants to join us. That way, we will have a small group. Re-tirement is a shared experience; it is best if both partners understand what is happening. Dave, it would be a good idea if you explained to Diane, Les, and his wife some of the things we talked about today - like re-tire with a dash and the new way of viewing re-tirement."

"That's great," said Diane. "We can meet at our house next Sunday."

"Sounds good to me," I said.

"Thanks for your help," said Dave. "I'm starting to feel a little better about re-tiremet. I'll call Les and fill them in on what we talked about."

"You're welcome, Dave. My fence and I both thank you. Let me know the time, and I will be there."

As I headed for the house, I looked back at my fence and realized I got a little carried away trying to make my point. Perhaps Tom Sawyer wouldn't be so proud of me after all.

CHAPTER SUMMARY

- The traditional definition of retirement is negatively charged, suggesting withdrawal, retreat, or going to sleep. The main problem is that this outdated image can become a self-fulfilling prophecy.

- Retirement is updated as "re-tire" (with a dash) and is defined as a career earned from and following work.

- To complete the image, a re-tirement career is an extension of your work and leisure careers. It is the best of both and the opportunity to do something worthwhile (as in work) and enjoyable (as in leisure).

- The main advice from our sample of retired doctors was to plan your time, which is what Life Goal Planning will enable you to do.

- The difference between work and re-tirement as a Central Life Focus is work generally involves one activity, while re-tirement may end up being comprised of several activities.

- Re-tirement is like winning a (modest) lottery. Your first concern is to make sure your money will last, and because you would not necessarily have to work, you would be concerned about what you would do if you didn't go to work.

Chapter 2

DO YOU WANT TO KNOW A SECRET?
(The Beatles, 1963)

Key to Re-tirement Happiness

The following Sunday, we met at Dave and Diane's house. Les and his wife Janice had arrived before me, and after the usual introductions, we sat outside on the patio. Dave had explained most of what he remembered from our conversation last weekend to the others.

To begin, I turned to Les and said, "I understand that you are re-tired. That's good; it means you are a professional. We can learn from your experiences."

"I don't think I have much to teach anybody," said Les.

"Don't be so sure," I replied. "As I mentioned to Dave last week, you can't truly understand what re-tirement will be like until you experience it. As a re-tiree, you are an expert, so we can learn from your experiences. How long have you been re-tired, Les?"

"About 18 months now," he replied.

"And what are your impressions so far?"

Les looked at Janice, smiled, and said, "I'm not too impressed. I'm enjoying it, but to tell you the truth, at least for me, it's not all that it's cracked up to be."

"What do you mean?" I asked.

"It's hard to explain," said Les. "I'm having a pretty good time, but there are times when, well, quite frankly, I'm bored. I never thought that would be a problem."

Then Janice said, "Have you heard the expression, I married him for better or worse but not for lunch? Well, there is some truth in that."

Dave looked over to me and smiled as if to say, 'You've got your work cut out for you.'

"Here's the situation," I said. "Dave and Diane want to learn about re-tirement, and Les and Janice are the experts. By the way, Janice, are you re-tired?"

"I only worked part-time but stopped when Les re-tired," replied Janice. "I could go back if I wanted. My housework is a full-time job. And you never re-tire from housework."

"That's very true," I replied.

I began by outlining my plan of action. "As I am sure Dave told you, today we will go through what I call Life Goal Planning. I covered most of the preliminary stuff with Dave last weekend, so today we will jump right into it. I have been running this workshop for many years and can assure you that it is easy to apply.

"The truth is," I said, "you already have a pretty good idea of how it works but in a different context. To start thinking about this process, imagine that it is the middle of a dreary winter. You decide to take a holiday in the sun to brighten things up. So, you go to a travel agent who greets you with a big smile and a warm handshake. After dispensing with the preliminaries, he asks you where you want to go. You tell him that you are unsure but thought about going to Florida. He pulls out a book of hotel listings, shows you a few photos of several hotels, and quotes the price, including return airfare. Then, after giving you a few minutes to read the descriptions, he asks, "Would you like me to book the holiday?"

"Now, let's look at a different agent. This agent goes beyond asking where you would like to go. She asks pertinent questions about your needs, likes and dislikes, interests, budget, and what you expect from your holiday. After determining these details, suppose she comes up with a different destination, a cruise that had never occurred to you. In addition, let's assume that a cruise turns out to be far superior to the original destination you had in mind.

"The difference between the two travel agents is how they determined your destination. The first agent failed to clarify your destination. He did not provide any service you could not find on a website or travel brochure. The second agent took the time to gather a clear understanding of your needs. She realized that your actual destination was not a specific city or location but satisfying your needs. Then, she found you a destination that would enable you to satisfy your needs.

"A travel agent's job is easy when defining the client's destination. Yours may take a little work. But it will be worth it because knowing where you are heading and clearly understanding your re-tirement destination or objective is a necessary starting point in your re-tirement career. Besides, if you don't know where you are heading, there is no point in setting out; you can't make any plans or corrections along the way, and how will you know if you get there? As I explained to Dave last weekend, how you perceive or look at re-tirement can influence how you approach it. So, everyone must have a clear understanding of their re-tirement destination."

I asked the group to think about where they want to go or hope to gain from re-tirement, and after a few moments of silence, Dave replied, "I guess you could say that I have no idea of where I am heading."

"Join the club," said Les.

There was a long pause, and Diane said, "We like to travel."

I replied, "We are looking for an objective or destination that could apply to all re-tirees."

RE-TIREMENT OBJECTIVE

Most people do not clearly understand their objective or destination in re-tirement. Based on my workshop experience, I estimate that only about one-third of pre-re-tirees have clear-cut, formulated re-tirement plans. When asked this question, the typical reply is to list activities such as travel, spending more time with the grandchildren, starting a small business, spending the winters in a warm climate, and so on. However, specific activities are not your objective. Travel, golf, hobbies, volunteering, etc., are activities or vehicles that some people use to reach their objective or destination in re-tirement. Another problem with focusing on activities is if, for some reason, you can't pursue a particular activity, you could have a problem.

We are looking for a re-tirement objective that applies to all re-tirees, regardless of age, sex, marital status, financial level, or type of occupation from which they re-tired. As I mentioned to Dave earlier, many people haven't truly thought out where they are heading in re-tirement either because they assume it will take care of itself or they don't know how to go about it.

To help them answer this question, I said, "The problem is, you are overlooking the obvious. The one re-tirement objective that everyone shares is to enjoy themselves. They want a life that is worthwhile, enjoyable, and purposeful."

"That's certainly true," said Janice.

"It's hard to disagree with this," I said. "This objective can apply at all stages of life; the only difference is in re-tirement, you have control over your life, and your chance of reaching this objective is greater.

"Concepts such as enjoyment, worthwhile, and purpose mean different things to different people. Some things that I consider enjoyable or worthwhile may not apply to you, and vice versa. Over the years of running hundreds of re-tirement workshops, I have learned that everyone is unique, and I try whenever possible to be value-free and not impose my likes and dislikes on others. Whether or not something is enjoyable, worthwhile, or purposeful depends entirely on the meaning these concepts have for you. Life Goal Planning is based on this assumption.

"Having established that your destination is to enjoy yourself," I continued, "the next question is, how will you get there? What must you do to ensure your re-tirement is worthwhile and enjoyable? As Dave and I discussed last week, although money is important, money alone will not guarantee re-tirement happiness. You may be well off financially, but this will not ensure that you will enjoy your re-tirement."

"I would agree with that," said Les.

To take this issue to the next level, I asked Dave for a few sheets of paper and asked everyone to write the heading 'Miss from Work' on the top of the page. I continued, "The question I would like you to consider is what you will miss from work when you retire. Les and Janice, because you are re-tired, think about what you miss from work. For example, you might miss contact with people or the stimulation. Don't include things you are quite happy to give up, such as office politics or working late."

I gave them a few minutes to complete their list, and then I pulled out a sheet with the survey responses to the same question about what they missed from work.

As they wrote their lists, I jotted a few notes on a sheet of paper and, after a few minutes, said, "Before we look at your lists, take a look at my list."

Figure 2-1

> Miss from Work
>
> Friendships
> Stimulation
> Challenge
> Purpose
> Identity

"How does it compare to yours?" I asked.

"It's practically identical," replied Les.

"Why do you think I was so clever and knew your answers beforehand?"

"I guess it's because you have done this before," said Janice.

"I certainly have. In fact, this is a brief version of the list compiled by asking our sample of re-tirees what they missed from work. Let's take a closer look at what we have. First of all, Dave and Diane, if you are concerned about giving up anything on your lists when you re-tire, or Les and Janice, if you feel you are missing anything, you can console yourselves knowing it is a common concern.

"To analyze your answers, thinking about what you would miss when you re-tire, you are listing your reasons for enjoying work. Work is enjoyable because it is a source of friendships, achievement, challenge, etc. However, the most important thing you can learn from your list is it identifies your needs satisfied by work. In other words, work is enjoyable because it satisfies your need for friendships, achievement, challenge, and so on.

"You have just made an important perceptual leap. Your focus has shifted from work as an activity to your needs satisfied by work. By focusing on personal needs, we can explain, for example, why two people could do an identical job, but one enjoys it more than the other. The activity is the same for both people, but it satisfies more needs for one person than the other. It also explains why work may have been more enjoyable in the past compared to today. It may have satisfied more needs in the past. The work may be the same today, but its ability to satisfy your needs, say for challenge and stimulation, may have diminished. We have to look at an activity's ability to satisfy our needs, to understand why it is or is not enjoyable."

MISS FROM DENTISTRY

Chart 2-1 includes what your re-tirement mentors missed from practicing dentistry, based on gender, followed by a few comments. Notice that 29% missed nothing. Although many of the items may not come as a surprise, the key to re-tirement happiness is to replace these satisfactions lost from dentistry.

Biggest "miss" are old friends, but making new friends is a challenge both my wife & I are embracing.

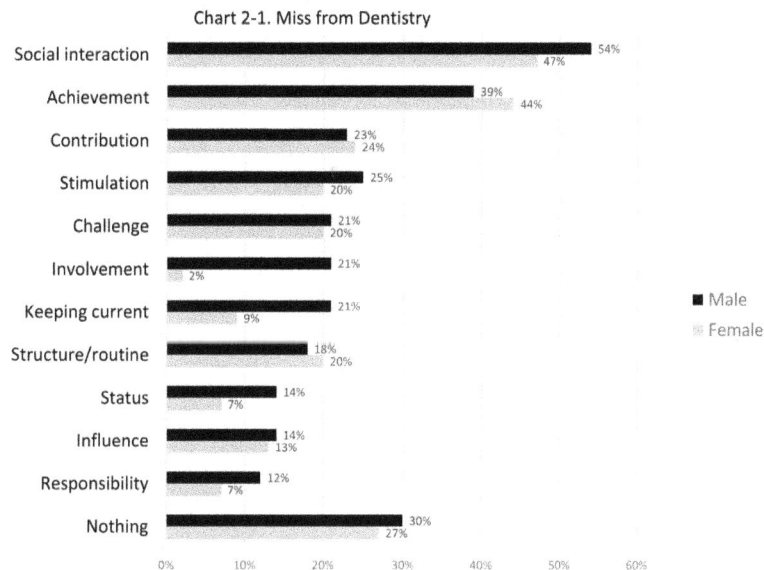

Chart 2-1. Miss from Dentistry

Category	Male	Female
Social interaction	54%	47%
Achievement	39%	44%
Contribution	23%	24%
Stimulation	25%	20%
Challenge	21%	20%
Involvement	21%	2%
Keeping current	21%	9%
Structure/routine	18%	20%
Status	14%	7%
Influence	14%	13%
Responsibility	12%	7%
Nothing	30%	27%

I am actually getting all of these in retirement building a Winery but maybe not as much interaction with people. I am a people person.

I cannot fully retire until I figure out how to replace the energy I get from work. I have saved enough money but energy is a perishable item. It can't be stored up in an account. Another concern is about becoming invisible. For 30 years I have been well respected.

I enjoy the balance of work/non-work that I have created. Still keeping the aspects of practicing that I like but without the stress of managing a practice.

I was ready for change so all the things that I enjoyed about practice were no longer important. Really appreciate my own time.

Thinking about what you would miss when you re-tire, you are in fact listing your reasons for enjoying work. Work is enjoyable because it is a source of friendships, achievement, challenge, and so on. However, the most important thing you can learn from your list is it identifies your needs satisfied by work. In other words, work is enjoyable because it satisfies your need for friendships, achievement, challenge, and so on.

You have just made an important perceptual leap. Your focus has shifted from work as an activity, to your needs satisfied by work. By focusing on personal needs, we can explain, for example, why two people could do the identical job, but one enjoys it more than the other does. The activity is the same for both people but it satisfies more needs for one person compared to the other. It also explains why work may have been more enjoyable in the past compared to today. It may have satisfied more needs in the past. The work may be the same today, but its ability to satisfy your needs, say for challenge and stimulation, may have diminished. So we have to look at an activity's ability to satisfy our needs, to understand why it is or is not enjoyable.

We were close to the point where I could reveal the secret to re-tirement happiness, but first, it was necessary to expand their understanding of the relationship between satisfying needs through different activities.

"Let's look at this from a different angle," I said. "Suppose a young person, we'll call him Michael, enjoys playing soccer. The question is, what is it about soccer that he likes? For example, he might like camaraderie and being with friends. Can you think of anything else he might like about soccer?

Les said, "I suppose the competition and the physical activity."

"OK," I replied. "Let's put this on paper. (Figure 2-2)"

Figure 2-2

Stage	Activities	Needs Satisfied
Child	→ Soccer	→ Friendships
		Competition
		Exercise
		Achievement

I continued. "As we discussed earlier, we can interpret Michael's reasons for enjoying soccer as his needs satisfied by soccer. In other words, he enjoys soccer because it satisfies his need for friendships, competition, exercise, and achievement. This reveals two important points. First, we enjoy activities because they satisfy our needs, and a single activity can satisfy more than one need. The more complex the activity, the more likely it is to satisfy your needs. Work, for example, generally satisfies many more needs than watching television. Yet even watching TV could satisfy more than one need, such as filling spare time, entertainment, and keeping up on current events. In addition, if you have absolute control over the remote, it can satisfy your need for power!

"Let's introduce another activity. Besides playing sports, Michael goes to school. This is a completely different activity, but if we include his reasons for enjoying school, Michael tells us that he enjoys learning, challenge, friends, and achievement."

I added this new activity to the original sheet (Figure 2-3).

Figure 2-3

Stage	Activities	Needs Satisfied
Child	Soccer	Friendships
		Competition
		Exercise
	School	Achievement
		Learning
		Challenge

"The main point is that some of Michael's needs can be met by completely different activities, while others may only be met by one activity. For example, his need for friendship and achievement are satisfied through soccer and school, while in our example, his other needs are only met by one activity. Of course, we could draw a line from sports to challenge. For other young people, the pattern may be different.

"To jump forward to the next life stage and look at Michael's needs satisfied by work, if we assume that Michael's needs satisfied by his work are similar to ours, here's what it looks like (Figure 2-4)."

Figure 2-4

Stage	Activities	Needs Satisfied
Child	Soccer	Friendships
		Competition
		Exercise
	School	Achievement
		Learning
		Challenge
		Money
Adult	Work	Stimulation
		Identity

"We see that some of Michael's needs were satisfied by work, some by soccer and school in the past, and others are unique to his current work. In addition, we could draw lines from soccer to learning, challenge, or status, or from school to stimulation, and so on. From here we conclude that different activities can satisfy the same need at different life stages."

"So far so good?" I asked.

They all nodded in agreement, so I continued. "The relationship between needs and enjoyment can apply to all activities. For example," I turned to Dave and said, "Say you and Diane went to a mall, and Diane enjoyed it more than you did. Can you explain why she enjoyed it more?"

"Easy," said Dave. "She has more money."

"Seriously," I said, "she might enjoy shopping at the mall more than you because it satisfies more of her needs than yours."

"That's for sure," said Dave.

"The same can be said for something you enjoy, Dave, but Diane doesn't. It may satisfy more of your needs than Diane's."

DEFINITION OF THE SITUATION

We can interpret these examples from the perspective of Situational Analysis (discussed earlier). As explained, people respond not only to the objective features of the situation but also to the meaning it has for them. Therefore, when Dave and Diane are at the mall, it is more enjoyable for Diane than for Dave because her definition of the situation (shopping) includes satisfying more needs.

We had reached the point where I could reveal the secret to re-tirement happiness. It should have been obvious at this point, so I asked if anybody could guess the secret based on what they had learned so far.

"Yes, don't let Dave and Diane near a shopping center," said Janice. "It's bound to end in a fight."

"That's one way of looking at it," I replied.

"Let me summarize what we have learned so far. Your objective in re-tirement is to enjoy yourself, and the reason we enjoy any activity is because it satisfies our needs. Many of our needs could be satisfied by a different activity at a different life stage, and when you re-tire, your needs satisfied by work will no longer be met.

"So, the key to re-tirement happiness is quite simple," I continued. "All you have to do is find alternative activities to replace satisfactions lost from work. That's all there is to it."

"In other words, you have to replace the word 'work' on this sheet with the word 're-tirement activities' - it may take more than one - and draw lines to the needs and skills you want to satisfy when you re-tire.

I included re-tirement on the sheet (Figure 2-5).

Figure 2-5

"With the freedom of re-tirement," I continued, "if you can satisfy more needs than those satisfied by work, life will be more enjoyable in re-tirement. On the other hand, if you cannot satisfy your needs lost from work, life in re-tirement will not be as enjoyable as life before re-tirement. In a nutshell, that is the essence of Life Goal Planning and the key to re-tirement happiness.

"I told you it was simple, and the beauty is, it works. Remember, your objective is not specific activities but to satisfy your needs, especially those lost from work. Re-tirement activities are simply vehicles through which you can satisfy your needs."

I waited for this to sink in and said, "What do you think? Does it make sense so far?"

Les was the first to respond. "It makes sense. I realize now that I was searching for things to do but didn't know what I was looking for. I didn't think about my needs. I took an art course but didn't enjoy it, and I'm a lousy artist. Somebody suggested I do volunteer work, but it doesn't appeal to me. A few of my re-tired friends seem to be having a great time. It's frustrating."

"It makes sense to me too," said Diane. "At the retirement (without the dash) seminar we attended, they talked about how important it was to find things to do in retirement. But they didn't explain it this way."

"Sounds good in theory," said Dave. "But how does it work in reality?"

"Now that you know the secret to re-tirement happiness and the theory behind the secret, I can give you an overview of a process designed to help you create a re-tirement that you will consider enjoyable and worthwhile."

IMPRESSIONS OF RE-TIREMENT

For an overview of re-tirement from the experience of our re-tired dentists, we can look at how satisfied they were with re-tirement, how they felt about the prospect of re-tiring just before they re-tired, and how they compared life after re-tirement to life before re-tirement. Starting with Chart 2-2, 95% were very or reasonably satisfied with re-tirement (59% +

Chart 2-2. Re-tirement Satisfaction

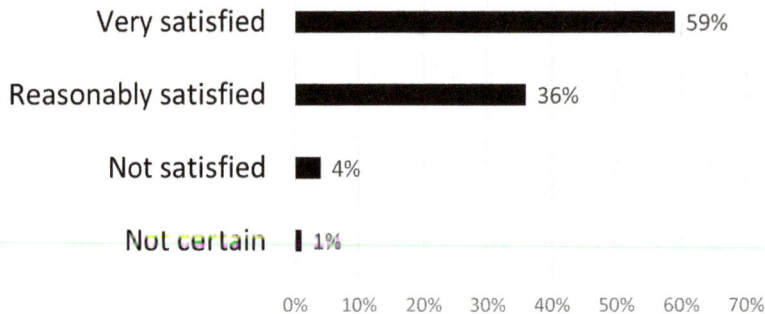

Very satisfied	59%
Reasonably satisfied	36%
Not satisfied	4%
Not certain	1%

0% 10% 20% 30% 40% 50% 60% 70%

Chart 2-3. Prospect of Re-tirement

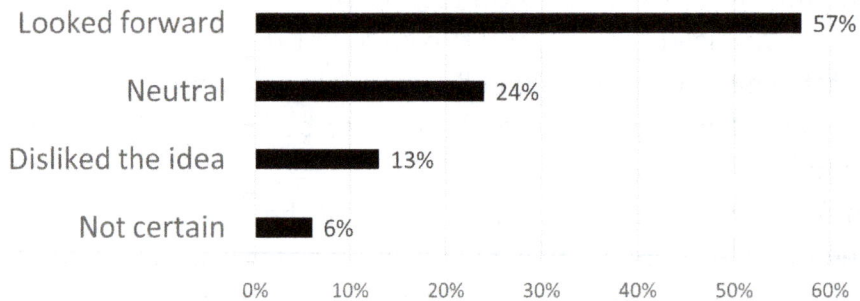

Looked forward	57%
Neutral	24%
Disliked the idea	13%
Not certain	6%

0% 10% 20% 30% 40% 50% 60%

36%). It also seems that opinions of re-tirement can actually improve after re-tirement, with slight variations by gender. Chart 2-3 indicates that only 57% actually looked forward to retirement before they re-tired. Yet after retirement, with some variation by gender (Chart 2-4), 93% felt that life was better or about the same in re-tirement. So it is it is possible that your impression of re-tirement will also improve after you experience it.

To gain a different perspective the survey included several open-ended or qualitative questions giving your re-tirement mentors free reign to elaborate on the main attractions and drawbacks of re-tirement. This perspective revealed several important underling issues and concerns that the quantitative responses had not necessarily identified. The responses to

Chart 2-4. Life Before and After Re-tirement

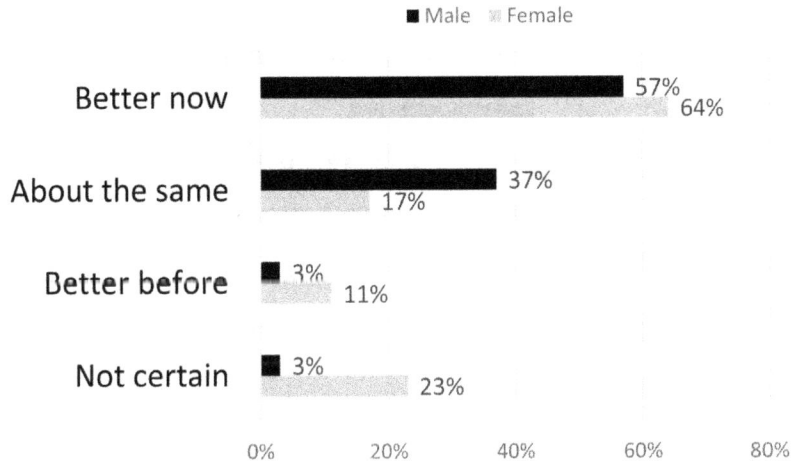

■ Male ▨ Female

Better now	57% 64%
About the same	37% 17%
Better before	3% 11%
Not certain	3% 23%

0%   20%   40%   60%   80%

each question ranged widely, but they present an excellent perspective from people with first hand re-tirement experience.

Re-tirement satisfaction can be influenced by many factors. So we cross tabulated retirement satisfaction with gender, health, marital status, and age. The only element that seems to have an effect among the subjects of our research, is health.

THE MAIN ATTRACTIONS OF RE-TIREMENT

When asked to describe the main benefits or attractions of re-tirement, they were presented with an open-ended question so they could respond without restrictions. This resulted in a very wide range of responses. But upon closer inspection, four main categories emerged (Chart 2-5). One that made general reference to the freedom and the opportunity to pursue your own thing. The other responses focused mainly on things they particularly enjoyed about re-tirement including the types of activities they pursued, in contrast to the things they were happy to give up from dentistry. The

Chart 2-5. Re-tirement Attractions

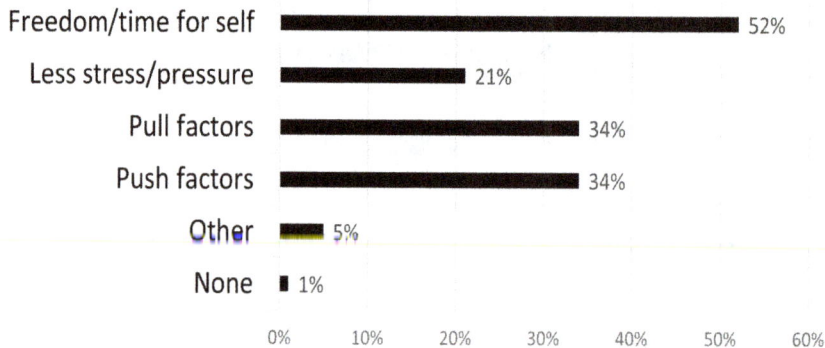

Category	Percentage
Freedom/time for self	52%
Less stress/pressure	21%
Pull factors	34%
Push factors	34%
Other	5%
None	1%

former can be classified as Pull Factors, or things that pulled them into re-tirement, while the latter represent Push Factors, or things that in a sense pushed them into re-tirement. Less Stress and pressures could be a push factor, but because it was mentioned by 21% of your re-tirement mentors, it was identified as a category on its own. To look beyond the number, here are a few direct quotes in each category.

Freedom

References to freedom implied the opportunity to do as you choose, which often stands in direct contrast to work.

For example:

Being able to do what you want, when you want to do it, without having to rely on other people. Having time to enjoy my family. Having time to improve my fitness. My time is my own.

Do what has to be done when it has to be done...OR NOT

Free time. Ability to concentrate energies on experiences and issues that I WANT to do, not that I have to do.

Freedom to thoroughly pursue the activities you could only do on weekends and holidays.

Time to do things that were put off due to lack of time.

To plan my day filled with what I want to do rather than plan around work schedules, planned time off, and needs of my patients. Spending time with family and activities I let go to focus on actively practicing dentistry.

Total independence from time constraints. Leisure time to spend with family and pursuing hobbies.

You now control your life and have given up all the responsibility.

PULL FACTORS

The pull factors include specific interests or activities the individual enjoyed pursuing in re-tirement. Some examples are; the opportunity to travel, spend more time with family, hobbies, sports, take on new or additional challenges, volunteer work, move to a new location, socialize, service clubs, and so on.

Able to travel at our convenience and for longer intervals without having to worry about getting back to 'the office'; time for children and grandchildren and the opportunity to help lighten their load AND to travel with their families !!

As long as you are healthy, it's an opportunity to pursue anything you want but it's a great opportunity to go back to school for any goal: pursue a hobby, learn something you have always wanted to do but had no time, 'second career....

Can ski when I want to! I can travel in Canada and USA during the year with our travel trailer. Have time to build and improve the house and time to invest in the markets.

Having the time and opportunity to follow desires with no time restraints. Fellowship of other retirees, totally different friends than when I was working. And more time to spend with my wife who is my best friend.

I always found that my job interfered with my hobbies. Now I have fixed that.

In my specialty it was not possible to travel for more than 2 weeks at a time. I can now travel whenever I want and for as long as I want. And I can spend 6 months at my home in California. I also have time for hobbies, sports and music.

More time with family, friends and colleagues Administrative responsibilities are minimal To continue to be of service to patients. Continue my education to provide current best practices for their care.

More time with friends and family. More time to travel Working on my sense of humor.

Pursuing hobbies without time pressures. in general taking things a bit slower. more time to be a grandparent.

Reading the paper, not just the headlines. Fewer mulligans, better golf. More soccer games and grand kids activities. More traveling.

Relaxation, travel without restrictions, hobby pursuit, visiting children, time with spouse, general freedom.

LEISURE IN RE-TIREMENT

For an overview of how your re-tirement mentors spend their leisure time, the activities they pursue are listed on Chart 2-6, separated by gender For insight into the varied nature of their leisure, here is a sample of activities identified as 'Other'.

Continuing studies on various topics through University and Public Library System.

Dental volunteering is a large part of my retirement.

Farm life and enjoying nature.

Having fun learning about investing and the stock market.

Hunting, fishing both sporty and commercial, Stock and option trading.

I decided to take a year off before committing to other passions.

Chart 2-6. Leisure in Re-tirement

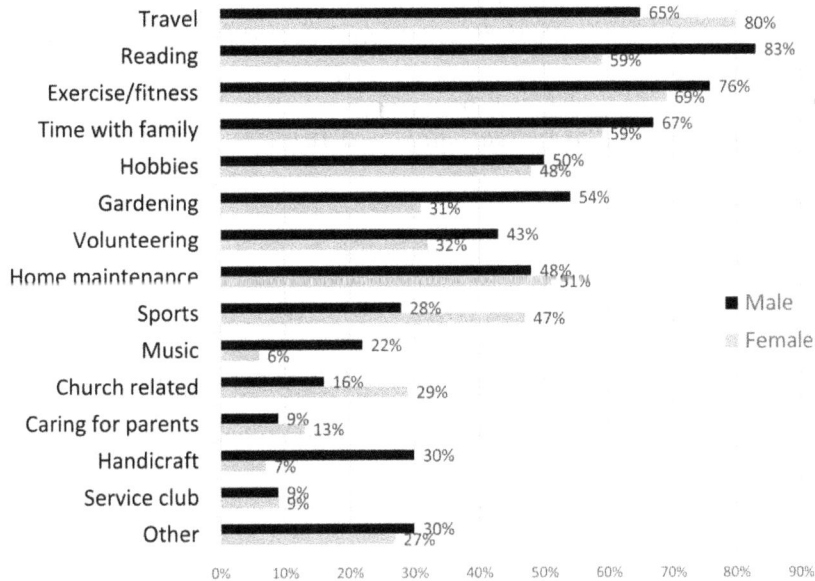

Activity	Male	Female
Travel	65%	80%
Reading	59%	83%
Exercise/fitness	69%	76%
Time with family	59%	67%
Hobbies	48%	50%
Gardening	31%	54%
Volunteering	32%	43%
Home maintenance	48%	51%
Sports	28%	47%
Music	6%	22%
Church related	16%	29%
Caring for parents	9%	13%
Handicraft	7%	30%
Service club	9%	9%
Other	27%	30%

I do some work as a certified life coach.

I have a 20 acre Haskap orchard that I maintain pretty much on my own.

I have been involved with dental testing agencies involved in licensing new dentists as an examiner

I have gone back to photography in a very meaningful way. Have been supporting numerous organization with material that is used on websites, print promotions, and instructional material. Have taken 2,000 to 4,000 images a week. My website has over 450,000 images produced in the past 14 years.

Kept my license and continued missionary work for two weeks a year. Exodontia in remote areas of developing countries. Let my license lapse three years ago. All done.

Learning Spanish language by self study books, tapes, and traveling to Panama. Currently live as an expat in Belize on an island.

Lectures and studies on numerous topics, attend theater and film.

Lucky to live in a beautiful, active, retirement community of 610 homes with many social and recreational opportunities.

Meditation, yoga.

Men's current events and investment interest groups.

Mission trips to foreign countries.

Most of my time is taken up with volunteering and creative writing. My wife and I travel a little, not much.

On-line university courses.

Part-time job as funeral director.

Play bridge on Internet and tennis 3 times a week. See grandchildren twice a week.

Playing with old cars.

Power boat racing, fishing, wood working

Practice brokering ,Ginseng farming, blackberry farming.

Real estate development.

RVing and boating.

Sailing, including trans ocean.

Search and rescue.

Serve on an international board and a Canadian board, a children's bible camp board, restorative justice, the Chamber of Commerce.

Shooting (handguns and rifles in nearby desert).

Spend most winters at a senior community in California. I participate in some group activities as well as manage the yard, cook, clean etc. Also management of my retirement investments.

Starting a Winery with my son and family, very busy!!

Taking language courses.

Teaching/coaching dentists.

Timber framing.

Took up golf as a new activity because it fulfills three key aspects of aging well, socializing, exercise, and learning something new.

Touring with my motorcycle around the United States and Canada!

Volunteer dentistry in foreign countries.

PUSH FACTORS

This category includes references to things about practicing dentistry that your re-tirement mentors were happy to leave behind. Things like, patient demands, responsibilities, shift work, government red tape, administrative tasks, and so on. As pointed in Chapter 6, it is preferable if your decision to re-tire was based more so on Pull Factors than Push Factors. Here are a few examples:

First time since Kindergarten that I have not had a schedule to meet/ run on all day. And kindergarten was a long time ago.

Freedom from a schedule Not dealing with employees and their problems. Freedom to pursue any interests I wish.

Freedom from the negatives of patient care...complaints, obligations, interruptions.

Having time to myself and not being a slave to a schedule and to people I might not like. Worry about overhead and staff interactions.

It is nice to not be concerned about all the regulations, staffing problems, management role, and being ultimately responsible.

Knowing that I no longer have to make all of the work related decisions on a daily basis. I also do not have to concern myself that health benefits are provided and worry about the ebb and flow of cash to cover all of the expenses related to private practice.

Less conflict, time to be unstructured, less sense of responsibility, not hurting people, able to try new things and experiences.

No responsibilities of running a business. No need to compete for patients and mange staff. Life is simpler and easier.

Not having to worry about office management. Not having to continually produce to cover the office overhead. I ran at a 52-55% cost, but that became increasingly difficult to maintain. Being able to spontaneously do something unrelated to work. Being able to stay at home when there was freezing rain. Mainly to be in control of my day and not be on the continuing grind of daily appointments.

LESS STRESS OR PRESSURE

I am enjoying the freedom from the daily stress of a private practice. I have time to do the things I enjoy at a pace I can manage.

Less stress and time to relax and plan your day.

Less stress from staffs and running an office.

Less stress. Less drama. fewer interactions with bureaucrats and insurance.

DRAWBACKS OF RE-TIREMENT

Re-tirement can have its drawbacks. To balance the equation, the survey included a question about the disadvantages of re-tirement. Replies to this question fell into six categories as on Chart 2-7, including 25% who said there were no drawbacks. We see that 41% mentioned social, and psychological losses that included boredom.

Chart 2-7. Re-tirement Drawbacks

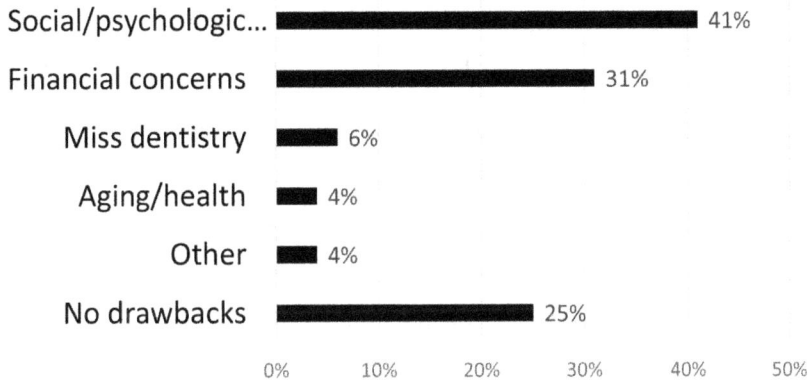

Category	Percentage
Social/psychologic...	41%
Financial concerns	31%
Miss dentistry	6%
Aging/health	4%
Other	4%
No drawbacks	25%

SOCIAL LOSSES

Giving up contact with patients and colleagues is another important drawback mentioned by our research subjects.

Really miss my patients and that social interaction. Really miss my staff and the fun related to all that we did. Miss the sense of purpose and being needed by our patients- Dentistry defines us to a great degree.

I miss the weekly interaction with my former staff and with the great people who were my patients.

Not being able to enjoy the company of the ninety percent of patients that were delighted with their treatment.

Miss having rapport with other dental staff and colleagues.

Missing the personal interactions with so many wonderful clients and some outstanding office team members

BOREDOM/KEEPING BUSY

Having too much time to relax and do nothing.

Losing the daily contact with patients. Losing the daily challenges of diagnosis and treatment. And the thanks of those who I have been able to help. Thus losing the satisfaction of a job well done. Also losing the structure of a well-organised day. I personally feel that adult happiness, well being, comes from useful work and accomplishment.

You have to be prepared to fill up those hours that your work occupied. It is difficult to get up and construct a game plan to fill up 24 hrs every day, after spending 25-30 yrs of having it all planned for you and just having to show up. Have some hobbies, interests, a "bucket list" and PLAN ahead to address these items that you would like to spend your retirement enjoying. Too many hours of nothing can make you reconsider your decision to retire. You have to be proactive.

PSYCHOLOGICAL LOSSES

This is a catch all category that includes many of the benefits we gain from work, besides money. These include lack of intellectual stimulation, reduced motivation, lack of identity, purpose, and so on.

A diminished feeling of accomplishment & being a worthwhile contributor to society.

I need to keep finding "projects" to keep me focused and creative.

lack of structure lack of project completion No longer having access to the energy people bring to the office.

Less stimulation for my brain. I need organization and structure. I need to feel I am making a difference.

The loss of patients' appreciation for the care you've given (less ego-feeding)

Unless you pursue a passion from before or one newly discovered you will rust and decay and fall into disrepair. Essentially challenges will appear to your physical, mental, spiritual, and emotional well being and whatever time you have left on this earth becomes a challenge sometimes overwhelming robbing you of the fullness this life has to offer. Nobody said this life was easy but for sure as you retire it can provide opportunities for your growth and happiness that you never envisioned as a loving and caring person and provide relationships anew and enrich others.

FINANCIAL CONCERNS

No matter when you re-tire - good times or bad - your income is likely to be reduced and you may have to learn how to budget your money.

Always wonder if there is enough savings to outlast my life span

Initially at least there is always the fear which may or may not be rational, about the amount of money needed /available.

Loss of office income. Typically get involved in more things and activities in retirement so costs do not go down but up.

Being dependent on volatile markets and puny interest returns for your income but this is overcome by living financially prudently.

MISS DENTISTRY

I loved my practice. I loved everything dentistry had to offer from the patient interactions, the challenges or remaining current with the ever changing improvements in materials and techniques and equipment to dealing with office and business administration. The challenges and joys of the staff relations which in most cases have ended in long lasting friendships.

I sometimes feel I am quite capable of doing dentistry and should be contributing in the way I practiced for year..

Missing the gratification of patients and the prestige of your position in the community combined with the self satisfaction of a case well completed.

AGING & HEALTH ISSUES

Several people mentioned health and aging as a drawback of re-tirement. This issue is discussed in detail in Chapter 7, so for now I will simply state that aging and health are not re-tirement issues. Think about it – if you never re-tired you would still grow older and perhaps have health issues. Sure re-tired people tend to be older, but keep in mind that re-tirement is defined as a career earned from and following work, and it has no effect on your age. Health and aging are physiological issues - not re-tirement issues.

I do not want to leave this chapter on a negative note, so as a reminder, 92% of your re-tirement mentors felt that life was better or about the same as life before re-tirement, and 94% were very or reasonably satisfied with re-tirement. If you are concerned about any of the drawbacks mentioned in this chapter, life goal planning can help you turn things around. In the meanwhile, keep your eye on the advantages.

CHAPTER SUMMARY

- Your main objective in re-tirement is that life will be enjoyable, worthwhile and purposeful.

- The reason we enjoy any activity is because it satisfies our needs. Often the same need can be met by a different activity, at the same or a different life stage.

- The key to re-tirement happiness is to find alternative activities that will continue to satisfy your needs and skills that were satisfied by your work.

- The main things your re-tirement mentors missed from dentistry included peer and patient interaction, a sense of achievement, contribution, involvement, keeping current and stimulation.

- The majority looked forward to re-tirement, felt that life in re-tirement was better or about the same as life before re-tirement, and were very or reasonably satisfied with re-tirement.

- The main attractions of re-tirement included freedom, the opportunity to pursue personal interests, and the absence of deadlines, stress or work responsibilities.

- The main drawbacks included financial concerns, social losses, and psychological losses such as feeling of boredom, lack of intellectual stimulation, lack of daily structure or routine, reduced motivation, lack of identity, purpose, and so on.

Chapter 3

TICKET TO RIDE
(The Beatles, 1965)

Life Goal Planning Overview

T his chapter includes a brief overview of the Life Goal Planning process. Complete instructions and worksheets are available in Part 2 at the end of the book. I recommend you read this chapter to understand the process and complete the workshop yourself or with a small group of friends/relatives.

Due to time constraints, I could not take them through the complete workshop. To give them a general understanding of the process, I began by saying, "To set the record straight, because everyone's needs and interests are different, Life Goal Planning will not tell you what you should do in re-tirement. What may appeal to me may not appeal to you, and vice versa. However, it will give you something much more valuable - the tools to make your re-tirement worthwhile and enjoyable.

"First, you must realize that the perfect re-tirement activities will not fall into your lap; it might take time to find them. When I refer to perfect, I mean activities that will replace your needs and skills lost from work. In addition, by referring to activities in the plural, I acknowledge that it may take several activities to accomplish this. Second, you may have to experiment with several different activities before you find the ones that are perfect for you."

To help them understand the process, I said, "When you go sailing, you know your destination. It could be across the lake, the ocean, or to return to where you started. What you don't know is the route you will take. If the winds are favorable and steady, you set the sails once and head straight for your destination. If the winds are shifting, which is usually the case, you have to tack or follow a zigzag course to reach your destination.

"The same process applies to Life Goal Planning. Remember, your destination is not a specific activity like travel, playing golf, or getting a job. Activities are vehicles through which you can satisfy your needs. Your destination or objective is to replace satisfactions (needs and skills) lost from work. If the conditions are favorable and your re-tirement plans or activities enable you to satisfy your needs and skills, you have reached your destination. You do not have to make any adjustments. If conditions are unfavorable and your plans do not satisfy all your needs and skills, you will have to experiment with different activities to reach your destination."

"Life Goal Planning involves several stages. So far, we have dealt mainly with concepts and theory. Now we will apply the secret to re-tirement happiness in the real world. Today, you will learn how to identify your needs and skills and evaluate activities based on those needs and skills. Dave and Diane, you can apply this to your future re-tirement plans. Les and Janice, you can apply this to your re-tirement. Then I will show you how to develop new plans before or after you re-tire."

PLANS IN HAND

Many people in my workshops know what they want to do when they re-tire. Well, that may be so. However, conditions may change, or what they thought would be worthwhile may be the opposite. Time and time again, I come across people who became disenchanted with re-tirement after the initial 'honeymoon' phase ended. They got the travel bug out of their system or found that playing golf every day was not as much fun as they thought it would be. So, whether you have plans for re-tirement or not, you must take the time to evaluate what you will do with yourself in the future - just in case.

Also, for people whose main occupation is housework, I acknowledge that one rarely re-tires from this line of work. Life Goal Planning is just as relevant. The only difference is to think in the context of housework rather than paid work. Occasionally, I have met a spouse with the attitude, and I paraphrase, "I am just here because of my husband." Re-tirement is a shared experience that can affect both partners. The more knowledgeable both partners are about re-tirement, the more likely the transition will be successful.

"OK, let's get started," said Les, anxiously.

To start the process, I said, "The first thing you must realize is that this process may take some time. Today, you may find an inspiration to serve you well throughout your retirement career. On the other hand, it is more likely that you will have to experiment with different activities until you reach your destination. Remember, you are attempting to replace satisfactions lost from work, which can be a tall order. Having said that, if you keep applying the Life Goal Planning process, you may be able to reach your destination sooner rather than later."

DEVELOP YOUR NEEDS AND SKILLS LIST

"Given that your objective or destination in re-tirement is to satisfy your needs and skills, especially those lost from work, your first task is to find out what these are. You must clarify your destination by developing a Needs and Skills List to determine exactly what you must replace. You can accomplish this by answering a few simple questions about your work and leisure. The complete program includes seven questions, and the more information you gather about your needs and skills, the more you have to work with. Today, we will look at three questions. This should give you a good start, and you can continue the process later.

"The first question focuses on needs at work. We looked at this earlier when I asked you to write down what you missed from work. If you recall, the things you might miss turned out to be your needs satisfied by work. Take a piece of paper and write the heading 'Needs & Skills' at the top left. Dave and Diane transfer your list of things you will miss when you re-tire, and Les and Janice transfer the things you miss in re-tirement to your new list. At the same time, you might add a few new things you hadn't thought of originally. Take a few minutes to do this exercise because these are the main things you may have to replace when you re-tire."

After allowing a few minutes to complete this question, I said, "When I spoke about replacing satisfactions lost from work, I was referring to both needs and skills. Your list must also include your skills because this is part of the reason we enjoy an activity. And because skills are transferable, you may use some of your work skills in a completely different re-tirement activity. Think about your skills at work and add them to your list under your needs satisfied by work.

"To help you think about your skills, sometimes we take our skills for granted because they may be second nature. So, imagine that you had to find your replacement when you re-tire and ask yourself what skills you would look for in your replacement."

After they added work skills to their lists, I said, "There is more to life than work, and if you are interested in uncovering your needs, you should also look at leisure. After all, you freely choose leisure activities, and we generally choose those we enjoy. Therefore, they can provide excellent clues to your needs. So, on the next line of your list, after your work skills, write down an activity you do for leisure, and then below that, list your reasons for enjoying that activity. Thinking about your reasons for enjoying leisure is very important because it identifies your needs satisfied by that activity. Do this for several leisure activities if you can. When you finish, I will show you how you can put your Needs and Skills List to work."

After a bit of discussion, they were ready for the second stage of the process.

"Although we haven't answered all the questions from my workshop (see all seven questions in the Appendix), you have created something valuable," I explained. "To prove this, let me ask you a question. How many of you would agree that if all the items on your list were met when you re-tired, your re-tirement would be worthwhile and enjoyable?"

In unison, they agreed.

"In that case," I said, "you possess something of value that most people do not have when they re-tire. You know your destination or objective in re-tirement. Your destination is to satisfy the items on your Needs and Skills List. Think of your list as a wish list for re-tirement. If you satisfy the items on your list, your re-tirement will be worthwhile and enjoyable."

EVALUATE RE-TIREMENT PLANS

The next stage involves using the list of needs and skills to evaluate re-tirement plans. Although the process is the same, it differs slightly if re-tired. I turned to Dave and Diane and said, "You now have a brief list of your needs and skills, and you agreed that if these items were met when you re-tire, then your re-tirement will be worthwhile and enjoyable. So now, you can use this as a benchmark to evaluate your plans. Les and Janice, you can use the same evaluation process to determine what is missing from your re-tirement.

"Here's how it works," I continued. "Dave and Diane, look at your list of needs and skills and ask yourselves if each item will be satisfied given your re-tirement plans. Go through each item and place a 'Y' next to those needs or skills that you expect will be met, an 'N' next to those that will not be met, and a question mark next to those that you are not sure of because you may have to wait until you re-tire.

"Les and Janice do the same, but because you are re-tired your evaluation will be based not on what you expect but on your current experiences. In your case, there will be no question marks. You don't have to wait to see if a need or skill will be met; you are retired."

I asked Dave and Diane if they identified a need or skill that would not be met when they re-tire.

"I found a few," said Diane.

"The problem is," said Dave. "I don't have any plans, so I don't have much to work with."

"That's OK," I replied. "Because soon I will show you how to develop new plans."

I turned to Les and Janice and asked the same question.

"I can see quite a few missing things," said Les. "It sort of gives you a whole new perspective."

"You can use this," I explained, "before or after you re-tire. This information or these insights may spark an idea of improving your plans or current activities."

IMPROVING PLANS

Many participants of my workshop have improved their plans as a result of this process. One example was a welder who planned to re-tire to a small farm and set up a welding shop. When he evaluated his plan to move to the farm, he identified 'teaching' as an item on his Needs and Skills List that was not part of his re-tirement plans. He identified teaching as a need during the brainstorming session, and given his welding skills, he started to think about how he could satisfy this need and thereby improve his re-tirement. Although this may seem obvious, he didn't consider this prospect until he evaluated his plans based on his Needs and Skills List.

Another was a couple who planned to move to the coast and buy a condominium in a high-rise building. When they reviewed their list of needs and skills, the husband loved gourmet cooking and identified items related to this interest. The wife identified items related to her love of antiquing. Their interests would be enhanced with their current plan. As they pondered their situation, and with help from other workshop participants, they came up with the idea of purchasing a small farm in the country. This would enable him to open a gourmet restaurant, and she could sell antiques. This idea opened new opportunities, including trips to Europe to purchase antiques.

BRAINSTORMING TO CREATE NEW PLANS

The next stage involves an entirely different process as a starting point for creating new plans. To explain, I said, "Now that you know how to evaluate your plans, it is time to learn how to come up with or create new plans. The perfect re-tirement activities that will satisfy your needs will probably not just fall into your lap. You may have to create them, and you must start somewhere. Les, you mentioned that you would like to find some new interests in re-tirement, and Dave, you are still pondering the question of what to do when you re-tire. So, let's look at these issues. You can use your Needs and Skills List as a starting point in both cases. This process works best with a small group, but you can do it on your own. It's based on brainstorming, and I will explain how it works with a group.

"The objective of the brainstorming session is to receive as many re-tirement suggestions as possible. Each person takes a turn to read their entire Needs and Skills List aloud. Meanwhile, the others take notes and jot down what they think are the reader's key needs and skills. Then look at your notes, and each person should come up with a re-tirement career suggestion for that person. When a suggestion is made, and this is very important, whoever receives the suggestion should write it on one sheet of paper headed 'Suggestions Received,' and whoever made the suggestion should write their suggestion on a sheet of paper headed "Suggestions Given." To start the brainstorming, I asked Les, our resident re-tiree, to read his list of needs and skills aloud and for the others to take notes as he read.

When Les finished reading his list, I said, "Based on Les's needs and skills, can anyone suggest what he might do to add something new to his life?"

Dave asked, "Les, you used to restore old furniture. Do you still do it?"

"Sometimes," Les replied.

"Then why don't you put an ad in the paper to restore furniture?" Dave suggested.

I interjected at this point and said, "OK, Les, you have a suggestion, so write it on your Suggestions Received sheet. Dave, because you made the suggestion, write it on your sheet headed Suggestions Given."

"If you say so," said Dave, but what's the use in me writing down his suggestion?"

"I will explain it to you soon," I replied. "Now, does anybody else have a suggestion for Les?"

Janice said, "Les, you could sell some of the stuff we have in the basement and garage."

Again, I reminded Les to write the suggestion on his sheet and Janice to write the suggestion on her sheet, which was headed 'Suggestions Given.'

Then Diane added, "Les, you mentioned public speaking as a skill. Why not see if you could teach a course on public speaking? Or maybe you could volunteer."

"These are all excellent suggestions," I said, reminding everyone to write the suggestion on the appropriate page.

During the brainstorming exercise, I asked them to put personal judgments and evaluations aside to allow ideas to flow. Now that each person had several ideas to work with, I let them in on an important secret that could be insightful for revealing additional needs and skills for their list and might help them find the perfect re-tirement. First, I asked them to take a close look at the suggestions they made to others and asked them what they saw. They spent a few minutes pondering this question, and then Les said, "Actually, I see a few things here that appeal to me."

"Me too," said Diane.

"The reason for this," I explained, "is when you make a suggestion to someone else, you are saying, if I were you, this is what I would do. So, giving suggestions to others turns out to be an excellent way to uncover additional interests and needs that apply to you."

"But the point is," I continued, "you are not the other person, but if you were, this is how you would approach it. Look closely at the suggestions you made for others. This might give you additional clues for your re-tirement. Do you see any patterns? Did you make several suggestions, such as starting a business, teaching, helping others, or joining something? If you see a pattern among the suggestions you made or any words that appeal to you, you have identified additional needs or skills that you can add to your list.

"Now look at the suggestions you received. If you identify a suggestion or even part of one that appeals to you, add them to your Needs and Skills List if they are not already on your list."

Next, we looked at how to tie this all together. I asked Dave for a pitcher of water and five empty glasses to demonstrate this process.

GUIDE YOUR RE-TIREMENT CAREER

To explain this process, I filled four glasses with varying amounts of water and arranged them on the table in a zigzag fashion. Then I filled the fifth glass, drank it, and set it aside. I was thirsty.

Figure 3-1

Plan A

Plan B

Plan C

Destination/Objective

As they looked on, I explained, "To demonstrate how your re-tirement career will develop based on your needs and skills, imagine that these four glasses represent your re-tirement career. The full glass represents your re-tirement objective - that is the point when you find activities that will enable you to satisfy your primary needs and skills, especially those lost from work.

"After you re-tire, suppose you pursue Plan A, or if you don't have plans, you start to pursue the idea from the brainstorming session that appeals to you the most. However, suppose you begin pursuing Plan A, and something is missing. You are not satisfying all your needs.

"Based on your experience in Plan A, you go back to your Needs and Skills List to determine what is missing. Then, as we did earlier, you brainstorm and develop a new idea. This leads you to Plan B. It satisfies more needs, but still, something is missing. Repeat this process until you finish at the full glass, where all your needs are satisfied.

"The key to this process," I emphasized, "is to understand that what you end up doing may be the furthest thing from your mind when you initially set out. However, because you did Plan A, which led to Plan B and C, you will ultimately reach your re-tirement destination where all your primary needs and skills are satisfied.

"When I refer to re-tirement as a career, that is exactly what I mean. It will develop and progress through several activities, all building from the last until you find the perfect re-tirement that satisfies your needs."

I presented a hypothetical scenario incorporating the various Life Goal Planning concepts to reinforce this point.

"Suppose my re-tirement plans - my Plan A – was to spend the winters in a warm climate, find a part-time job to top up my income and take up tennis with my wife. I expect that these plans will satisfy my needs. Then, suppose it doesn't quite work out when I pursue my plan. I look for a part-time job but can't find anything interesting. Although we enjoy being away in the winter, I am a bit bored, and while playing tennis, I sprained my ankle.

"Something is missing from my life, and I am at the glass that is only partially full."

"Sounds a bit like me," said Les.

Janice smiled and asked for a glass of water. Dave and Diane laughed at this request.

To continue with my hypothetical scenario, I said, "To improve my situation, I return to my Needs and Skills List to see what is missing. Suppose I identify friendships as missing. My ankle has healed, so we joined a tennis club to meet new people and take tennis lessons. While at the tennis club, we met a couple, and they invited us to go hiking. This idea didn't occur to us before, but we decided to join them. We had a great time with their group on the hike, so we quit the tennis club and spent most weekends hiking either with the group or just the two of us. I have reached the next glass through my revised plans. I satisfy more needs, including the need for friendships.

"I have become heavily involved in the world of hiking. I developed a website on hiking that I can access when I am away in the winter. It includes an active chat room, and I started to organize hiking trips to exotic locations. Now, we travel to scout out potential hiking trips. My cup, or my glass, runneth over. I have reached my destination and am satisfying all of my needs. In fact, I am satisfying more needs than before I retired.

"The main point of my example," I continued, "is the activities that I ended up doing in re-tirement were the furthest things from my mind when I re-tired. If somebody had suggested that I develop a hiking website, I would have said they were crazy. Nevertheless, because I sprained my ankle, we joined a tennis club, met a couple of hikers, and so on.

"So, start by picking an activity. It doesn't have to be perfect, but you must start somewhere. Evaluate it with your Needs and Skills List. If it seems like a good idea or if it seems like it will satisfy most of your important needs, go for it. You will never know unless you try. If it doesn't work out or conditions change, brainstorm a new idea based on your current pursuits, evaluate it, and move on to something better. Continue this process until you reach your destination that satisfies most if not all of your needs and skills."

As I explained, "Your Needs and Skills List can be valuable before and after you re-tire. It can be used to evaluate plans or ideas, to come up with new ideas, and to make adjustments as you progress through your re-tirement career."

"I follow what you are saying," said Janice. "I have a friend, Barbara - you know her, Diane. When they re-tired, she and her husband wanted to travel and spend some time living in a foreign country. Unfortunately, her husband became ill, and they couldn't travel. What should they do then?"

"That's an excellent question," I replied. "Like the song says, you can't always get what you want. Right now, what I want is to take a little break. Let's return to this in a few minutes if you don't mind."

YOU CAN'T ALWAYS GET WHAT YOU WANT
(Rolling Stones, 1969)

After a short break, I recalled Diane's question and said, "I agree with you, Diane. It's all very well to talk about finding enjoyable and worthwhile pursuits in re-tirement, but what if you couldn't do what you wanted for some reason? Suppose you wanted to find a job but couldn't. Suppose your dreams included sailing, but your spouse must be on dry land for medical reasons. What if you wanted to travel but couldn't afford it?"

I answered my question. "You can get what you want if you find an alternative way. Remember, finding a job, sailing your boat, or traveling are not your objectives. Your objective is to satisfy your needs. A job, sailing, and travel are activities or vehicles through which you can satisfy your needs. You can meet the same need or skill through different activities. So, if you can't go sailing or find a job, determine which needs you would like to satisfy and find or create an alternative activity that will allow you to satisfy most if not all of those needs."

I told them about a couple from a workshop who wanted to move to the coast and spend time sailing their boat when they re-tired. That situation was similar to her friend Barbara's. Unfortunately, just before they were about to move, the wife fell ill, and her doctor advised against this plan. They were devastated. What could they do? They had been planning this move for a long time.

They had two options. They could abandon their plans and do nothing or look for an alternative. Realizing that they planned to satisfy certain needs and skills, they sat down and identified those needs and skills. Then, given the wife's medical needs, they brainstormed an alternative and decided to buy a trailer and travel the coast. Although their alternative was not quite as ideal as sailing, it was another way they could satisfy most of their travel needs, including the additional need for immediate access to health care, if necessary.

This is an important point, so I followed up with another example.

"Remember I mentioned a welder who improved his re-tirement plans when he identified teaching as one of his needs? Suppose after he moved to the farm, he approached the local school to teach welding. Suppose the school didn't need a welding teacher. What do you suggest he should do?" I asked.

"He could look for another job," said Les.

"That's true," I replied. "But suppose his needs were focused more on teaching than earning money. He wasn't after a job. He wanted to pass his skill on to someone else."

"Maybe he could teach somebody on his own," suggested Diane. "You said that he was going to open his own workshop. That would be perfect."

"Good suggestion, Diane," I said. "His main concern was to satisfy his need to teach. If he can't do it through school, he may be able to find an interested kid who would love to learn how to weld, and he could teach them on his own. On the other hand, maybe teach something else altogether. If his need to teach welding in a school was great enough, he may go back to school and become a teacher. Who knows? Remember, re-tirement is a career that will develop and evolve; sometimes, you never know where you will end up."

ACE UP YOUR SLEEVE

"The point is," I emphasized, "You have an ace up your sleeve. If you want to do something but can't do it for some reason, you have the tools to find or create an alternative. You do not necessarily have to rely on others as you progress through your re-tirement career. This is in stark contrast to the work career experienced by most people.

"Say somebody wanted to find a job or had a job and hated it. The same needs may be satisfied through self-employment or a nonpaying activity. If you can't afford to travel, you can organize a group and maybe have your way paid for by a travel agency. On the other hand, you might travel on a freighter or find something completely different - if it satisfies your needs. If, for some reason, you are unable to pursue anything, the process I described earlier will allow you to create a worthwhile and enjoyable alternative. Who knows, your alternative may be a blessing in disguise. It may turn out to be better than the original.

"Looking for a job is like looking for any activity in re-tirement. The only difference is that a job satisfies (in varying degrees) an extra need, which is money. Remember," I added, "your destination or objective is to satisfy your needs. If you can't participate in one activity, find an alternative activity to satisfy those needs. This simple fact is at the heart of a successful re-tirement career. You have the time, and now you have the tools to create a future that will be worthwhile and enjoyable. All you have to do is put them to work."

CHAPTER SUMMARY

- Given that the key to re-tirement happiness is to replace your needs and skills satisfied by work, the first step in Life Goal Planning is to identify your needs and skills, i.e. create your Life Goal List.

- Your Life Goal List identifies the conditions to make your re-tirement worthwhile and enjoyable.

- This creates a benchmark against which you can test your re-tirement plans to identify a Life Goal shortfall and perhaps improve your plans.

- Your Life Goal List can also be used to compare different plans and determine which one is likely to satisfy more of your needs and skills.

- If new plans are necessary, your Life Goal List can be used as a basis or starting point to brainstorm new ideas.

- Finally, you can use your Life Goal List to guide your re-tirement career so that eventually your re-tirement will be worthwhile and enjoyable.

- If you want to do something but can't do it for some reason, you have the tools to find or create an alternative activity that will satisfy your needs.

Chapter 4

A HARD DAY'S NIGHT
(The Beatles, 1964)

Working in Re-tirement

Working in re-tirement is not for everyone. However, it is not uncommon for people to think about this prospect. Even if you do not plan to work in re-tirement, this issue can provide insights into your re-tirement career. Before we deal with this issue, let's look at your re-tirement mentors.

Forty-four percent of your re-tirement mentors worked for a salary or other compensation since re-tiring. However if we separate the respondents by their location, there was a tendency for the U.S. respondents to be more likely to work in re-tirement compared to their Canadian counterpart (53% vs. 33%). In general, 90% worked part-time and 81% worked in dentistry related activities. To look a little deeper, there are various reasons why people seek work in re-tirement. On the one hand, some may have felt a financial pinch in re-tirement and felt the need to earn extra money. On the other hand, some may have felt bored and looked for work to relieve this situation.

To test these differences, those people who worked in re-tirement were asked if their reasons for working were mainly financial or non-financial. And we find that only 12% worked in re-tirement strictly for the money. Table 4-1 confirms the non-monetary benefits as reasons for working in re-tirement. This is also consistent with the things they missed from work as

Chart 4-1. Reasons for Working in Re-tirement

Reason	Male	Female
Social interaction	78%	76%
Stimulation	71%	59%
Satisfaction	75%	71%
Having something to do	48%	35%
Challenge	44%	41%
Routine	21%	19%
Strictly money	12%	12%

■ Male
▪ Female

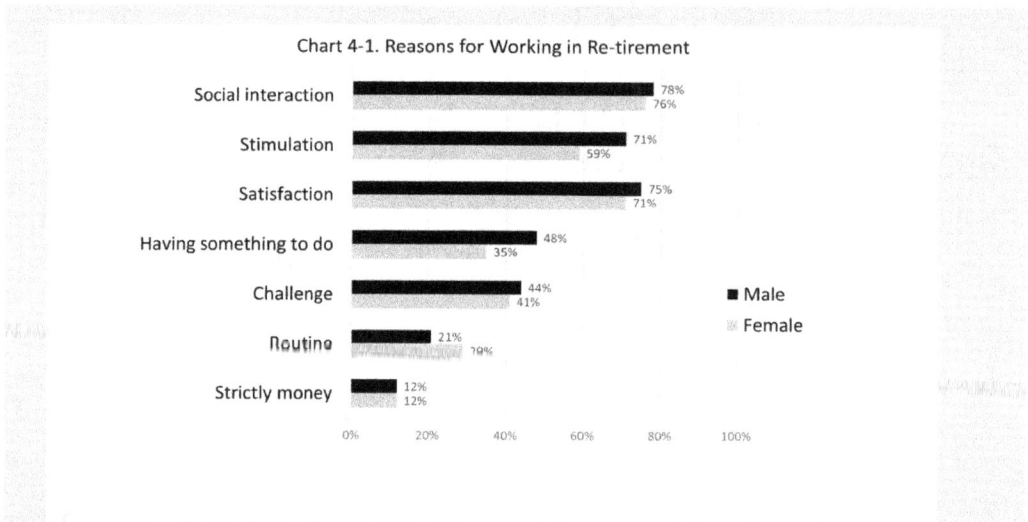

outlined in Chapter 2, namely, peer and patient interaction, achievement, challenge, and so on. We can conclude, therefore, that working in re-tirement usually serves as a vehicle to replace non-monetary satisfactions lost from work.

Here are a few comments as reasons for working in re-tirement.

Because I was asked to work as a dental consultant for an auto insurance program.

Continuing to contribute, maintain connection with youth and technology.

Doing locums several times in a year for a past associate.

Helping daughter with business management in her practice.

Helping hygiene students locally or dental practitioners in third world countries benefit from the experience that I have accumulated over my career.

Helping out a friend in his business where I had previously volunteered.

I have done a couple of locum as favors to friends.

Managing investments.

Mentoring/teaching dental students.

To expand on the finding that working in re-tirement usually serves as a vehicle to replace non-monetary satisfactions lost from work, we looked at the relationship between re-tirement satisfaction and working in re-tirement. From Chart 4-2, we see that there was not a signification difference between those who worked and those who did not work in re-tirement. Nevertheless, working in retirement is motivated by non-financial rather then financial factors.

Chart 4-2. Working and Satisfaction

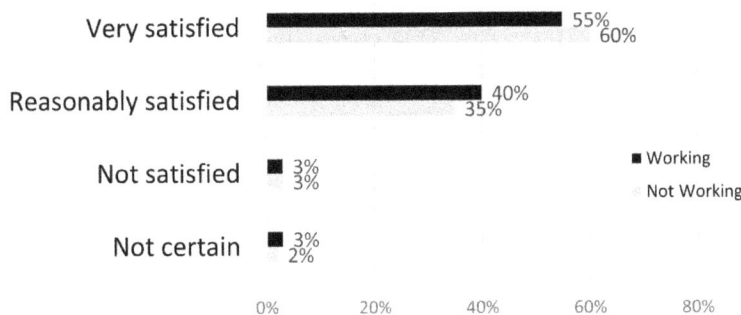

Very satisfied	55% / 60%
Reasonably satisfied	40% / 35%
Not satisfied	3% / 3%
Not certain	3% / 2%

■ Working
Not Working

0%   20%   40%   60%   80%

POSTPONING RE-TIREMENT

Here is something to ponder. One would assume that working in re-tirement was a function of economic conditions. As conditions worsened, more people would be likely to work in re-tirement. Several research studies carried out after the financial meltdown in 2008 identified a high percentage of workers planning to postpone their re-tirement. For example, the Transamerica Retirement Survey in 2012 found that 60% of the respondents over age 60 plan to work full or part-time when they retire.[1] A survey by the Employee Benefit Research Institute[2] put this figure at 70%, while a study by SunAmerica found that 65% want to include some work in retirement.[3] A Canadian survey in 2012 found that 53% of people in their 50's plan to work in retirement (CIBC Retirement Survey).[4]

If we look at this issue before the economic meltdown, we are in for a bit of a surprise. In 2004, one study found that 75% of older workers said that it's at least likely that they will work for pay after they retire[5] and in 2006, another study reported that 77% expect to work for pay after they retire.[6] We can add to this that 43% of your re-tirement mentors actually worked for a salary since re-tiring before the economic meltdown. In other words, there does not seem to be a direct link between economic conditions and wanting to work in retirement. There must be something more to postponing re-tirement than meets the eye.

The answer lies partially in the reasons for wanting to postpone re-tirement. When the subjects of the 2004 study were asked why they wanted to work in re-tirement, they focused mainly on non-financial issues, including staying mentally alert (93%), feeling useful (74%), and social interaction (86%). The least mentioned reason was that they needed the money (44%). The 2006 study reported that most wanted to work "because they'll want to, not because they'll have to."

Financial conditions have influenced the decision to work in re-tirement since 2008. However, the non-financial reasons also had a significant effect. For example, in the TransAmerica 2012 study cited above, 41% planned to work because they enjoyed it or wanted to stay involved. In the Canadian survey, only one-third of those who plan to work post-retirement said they would do so just for the money and two-thirds — or 67% — saw working either as a way to stay socially active or that they just found work enjoyable and wanted to stay involved in the workforce in some capacity.

Therefore, it is safe to assume that many of your re-tirement mentors found work in re-tirement because they wanted to and for non-financial reasons, not because they had to for financial reasons.

Dave mentioned that he might consider looking for other work when he re-tires, so I asked him what type of work he was considering.

"I haven't decided on this yet," he replied.

"If you recall, last week when we talked, I mentioned that under the old definition where retirement without the dash was defined as withdrawal from work if somebody went back to work, they were referred to as semi-retired, which I guess means 'sort-of-retired' or 'half-retired.' By defining re-tirement as a career earned by and following work, working in re-tirement does not require a special label. Today, it is quite common."

Even though Dave had not decided about working, I wanted to give him something to think about - to help him decide. I told the others that most of what I had to say about working also applied to non-work activities.

TAKING THE EASY WAY OUT

"First of all, Dave," I said, "like most re-tirement issues, I can't tell you what to do. For some people, working in re-tirement is the best course of action, and it can be the opposite for others.

"Having said that, I highly recommend that as part of the decision process, ask yourself a fundamental question. Try to be honest with your answer. In your desire to replace satisfactions lost from work, are you taking the easy way out by going back to work?"

"What do you mean?" he responded.

"Well, have you thought seriously about why you are considering returning to work when you re-tire?"

"Sure I have," he replied.

"My skills are fairly marketable, but something in me pushes me to think about doing something completely different. However, I don't know what it could be. Besides, Diane doesn't want me hanging around the house. I have to find something to do when I re-tire."

"That sounds like good reasoning," I said.

I asked the others if they could think of other benefits to working in re-tirement.

"It allows you to be with other people and can be stimulating," suggested Diane.

"Absolutely," I replied. "We talked about this earlier. Besides money, work can satisfy many needs, including friendships, routine, getting out of the house, challenges, stimulation, identity, and so on. Some people work in re-tirement because they need the money. Others go back to work to satisfy these additional needs. There is nothing wrong with this, provided you consider it worthwhile and enjoyable and that it satisfies your other needs. If it didn't turn out this way, I take back my endorsement.

"If a person had to earn extra money, it might be necessary to ignore the non-monetary needs to satisfy the need for extra income. So, Dave, before you rush out to look for a job, pause and take stock of your situation. As I am sure you know, working can have some potentially negative consequences besides its positive benefits."

"I realize that," said Dave. "And that's why I am having a problem deciding."

"Let me tell you about Mark, who I met in a workshop. He worked for a government agency, and because he had been with the agency most of his working life, he would end up with a good pension when he re-tired. Anyway, during our workshop, he talked about his love of history. He would have loved to pursue this years ago but had to give it up to earn a living. When I asked about his re-tirement plans, he said he would look for a part-time job.

"I was somewhat surprised because re-tirement would be the perfect time for him to pursue his long-lost dream. If not now, when? I didn't know all the details; maybe he had to work, or he may have been afraid to return to school. Whatever his reason, it seemed he was giving up the perfect opportunity to pursue his dream. He may have been taking the easy way out by returning to work.

"The problem is, working in re-tirement is not necessarily a magic panacea. It can have a downside. Although it may satisfy some of your needs, such as earning money, working in re-tirement can impose restrictions and may not satisfy all your important needs. And as we all know, the key to re-tirement happiness is to satisfy your important needs."

EVALUATING WORK

To help evaluate whether working was Dave's best solution, I told him to look at his Life Goal List and identify the five most important needs or skills that must be satisfied when he re-tires. I asked him to think about each item, to be honest, and list these items on a separate piece of paper.

When he completed his list, I asked, "Did you include money?"

"Yes," he answered.

Then I said, "If you had to identify two items in your top five list that must be part of your re-tirement, would earning money be one of them?"

"Probably not," he replied.

"In that case," I asked, "would you agree that money is not your main motivation for working in re-tirement?"

"I don't know," said Dave. "Right now, things look OK, but you never know what will happen in the future. The stock market is unpredictable, so the financial side is critical."

"I am not denying that," I replied, "but there are many more things to consider when deciding to re-tire or whether or not to work in re-tirement."

To help him think about this decision more clearly, I suggested that he imagine or think about working for somebody and ask himself if the items on his Needs and Skills List, especially his top five needs, would be met. I acknowledged that this may be difficult now and that he may have to wait until he finds a job in re-tirement.

I suggested he add additional needs that did not appear on his original Needs and Skills list. These could include sleeping in, spending time with Diane, not being tied down, and so on. This exercise would also give him a better idea of what type of activity to look for. For example, if stimulation or spending more time with Diane were high on his list of priorities, he should bear this in mind when deciding about working in re-tirement.

"If you start to work," I continued, "and if things are not going well, don't forget that you have an ace up your sleeve. Consider this as one step in your re-tirement career. You have the tools to get you to the next step.

You may discover an idea that may never have occurred to you had you not started to work. So even if it doesn't work out, you may be able to benefit from it."

POSTPONING OR WORKING IN RE-TIREMENT

There are several issues to think about regarding working in re-tirement. First, suppose you apply for a job and are turned down. You may not be too concerned if it happened once. However, applying for several jobs and still turning up empty can affect your self-worth or esteem. Before you re-tire, you probably have a strong sense of self-worth and feel valued as an employee. But if several potential employers reject you, you may begin to feel down. I am not suggesting that you will not find a job. I have no way of knowing your value in the workforce. But if you experience several rejections, don't take this to heart - it is a fact of life that does not necessarily reflect on you. Finding a job can be difficult for anyone at any age or stage in life, but it can be especially problematic for a re-tiree.

If you feel that you must make up a re-tirement shortfall by continuing to earn money, is it preferable to postpone or work in re-tirement? You could argue that this difference is semantic because if you are working in re-tirement, you have postponed your re-tirement, and vice-versa. However, for our purposes, they are different. The former refers to retaining the status quo and continuing your current job or work. In contrast, the latter refers to re-tiring and finding some way to earn extra income in re-tirement, like finding a full-time or part-time job or creating your money-making venture. To return to the question above, the choice between postponing or working in re-tirement depends on if you can stay where you are, how much of a financial shortfall you need to make up, and where you can satisfy more of your needs.

If you cannot stay where you are, for example, if you lose your job, the decision has been made for you, and if necessary, you will have to increase your income through another source. The next consideration, how much of a financial shortfall you must make up, is very important. If, for example, you only have to make up a small portion of your re-tirement income, it may not be necessary to postpone your re-tirement, especially if your work does not satisfy your primary needs. At the same time, if you decide to look for work in re-tirement, you might consider part-time rather than full-time work.

There is nothing wrong with postponing or working in re-tirement, providing it enables you to meet your Life Goal. The extra income is a bonus. However, if it does not allow you to satisfy your needs, and you do not have to earn extra money, it's time to reconsider your options. That may not necessarily mean giving up the idea of working; it might mean working for you rather than others. Even though this option may not be for everyone, we can look at it in more detail. This means that when looking for work, you have to be creative and open to new ideas and opportunities.

If you are seeking a job or planning to start a business venture after re-tirement, you will need a plan of action that involves taking a series of steps. Depending on your marketable skills, preparing yourself is key to finding a job. Many people have marketable skills that can be used. Even if you have a marketable skill, this should not prevent you from trying something new. Often, you can transfer your skills to other areas. Learning a new skill does not diminish with age. All you need is the desire and a little research to select those that appeal to you and have the highest marketability. Check with your local school board or college for night classes. You may be surprised at what they are offering. You can also consider taking a course by either correspondence or attending a college or university.

Don't let your age inhibit you when looking for a job. Every reliable survey has shown that older employees are more dedicated, dependable, conscientious, and have less absenteeism than younger workers. They require less supervision, take their jobs more seriously, and have a greater sense of responsibility and loyalty to their employers. Their experience, more acute judgment, and maturity make them more efficient.

Before you apply for a job, imagine doing it and evaluating that job against your Needs and Skills List. If you get the job and it does not turn out to be all you expected, assess it again to find out what is missing. If it does not meet your primary needs and skills, you might consider moving on to something else. Unless you have to earn money, don't waste your re-tirement doing something you don't enjoy (i.e. that doesn't satisfy your most important needs and skills). Unless it is essential, do not sacrifice other needs for the need for money. If money is not imperative, you might consider looking for a non-monetary activity to satisfy your other essential needs. Alternatively, if the need for money is important, and you can't find a worthwhile and enjoyable job, you may have to create an activity that earns money. That is what Life Goal Planning is all about.

CREATE A MONEY-MAKING VENTURE

If you cannot find a job in re-tirement, you do not necessarily have to abandon your thoughts about work or earning money. You can focus on creating a money-making venture. The main advantage of this option is that you may be able to satisfy more needs than you would have if you postponed your re-tirement or found another job. If you only have to make up a portion of your re-tirement income, if your current work fails to satisfy your Life Goal needs, or if you cannot postpone your re-tirement, you might consider looking into ways to earn that portion in re-tirement and at the same time, you may be able to satisfy your Life Goal.

Creating a money-making venture can start with the brainstorming exercise (overview in Chapter 3, details in the Appendix), and you have to start with an idea or an inspiration that will develop and evolve through imagination, insight and experience. You are looking for suggestions that satisfy the items on your Life Goal List, but with the added condition that the suggestions satisfy your need for extra money. Start by brainstorming (alone or in a group) some small money-making ideas. It would be good to include others in the process as they may come up with an idea that may not occur to you. Do this for a while and select the most appealing suggestion that does not require a major investment. Start to investigate it, talk to people, maybe volunteer in that area, and do anything to get more insight into your initial idea. You may learn something about another approach you were unaware of initially. Be creative, think, ask around, experiment, and learn. Remember, re-tirement is a career, and to find a money-making venture, you have to start somewhere, so keep your eyes and ears tuned to new ideas.

WORD OF WARNING

It goes without saying that if you plan to invest in a business venture when you re-tire, ensure you do your due diligence and check it out thoroughly. I have met a few re-tirees who were relatively comfortable financially and bought into a business that eventually failed because they were bored. I am not privy to the financial issues involved, but you mustn't rush into something before checking it out thoroughly. In your desire to 'get back to work,' don't risk your financial reserves because it may be difficult to make up your losses.

CHAPTER SUMMARY

- Forty-four percent of your re-tirement mentors worked for a salary or other compensation since retiring.

- Ninety percent worked part-time, and 81% worked in dentistry related activities.

- Only 12% work strictly for the money. Reasons for working focused on social interaction, stimulation, satisfaction, and having something to do.

- The relationship between satisfaction and working in retirement was not significant.

- Other research confirms that the main reason people work in retirement is not necessarily for money, but for other satisfactions.

- There's nothing wrong with working in retirement as long as long as you consider it to be worthwhile and enjoyable - or unless of course it is necessary. But sometimes people consider work necessary, because they do not have any other alternatives.

- Creating a money-making venture could be an alternative, but as a word of caution, make sure you do your due diligence first.

Chapter 5

(MONEY) CAN'T BY ME LOVE
(The Beatles, 1964)

Financial Planning With a Dash

I am not a financial planner; my experience lies with the non-financial side of re-tirement education. Having said that, I have worked closely with many financial planners and advisers over the years, conducting re-tirement education workshops. It appears to me that financial planning on its own is not re-tirement planning; it is money management planning. I would argue that Life Goal Planning is the missing element that can transform financial planning into re-tirement planning. People spend both time and money in re-tirement, so complete re-tirement planning requires both Life Goal and financial planning.

Considering the importance of planning for re-tirement, the survey included a few questions on this issue. First, we see that only 34% received pre-tirement planning assistance before they re-tired. When asked who provided the assistance, 92% used a financial planner, 28% mentioned self-study, and 25% attended workshops or seminars. Regarding the content, it was predominantly financial planning (Chart 5-1). And when asked about areas where they could have given more attention (Chart 5-2), the majority felt that they were fully prepared. Another interesting issue is to compare retirement satisfaction between those who did and did not receive any pre-re-tirement planning. As Chart 5-3 reveals, there were no significant differences.

Chart 5-1. Re-tirement Planning Content

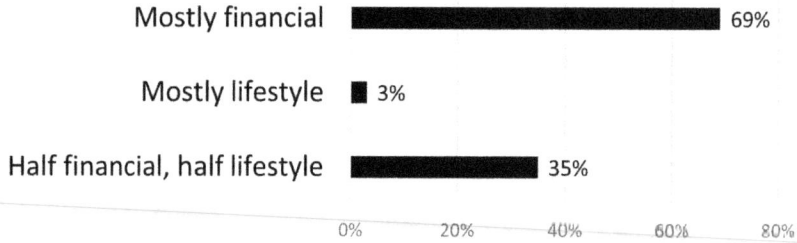

Mostly financial — 69%

Mostly lifestyle — 3%

Half financial, half lifestyle — 35%

0%   20%   40%   60%   80%

Chart 5-2. More Attention Needed

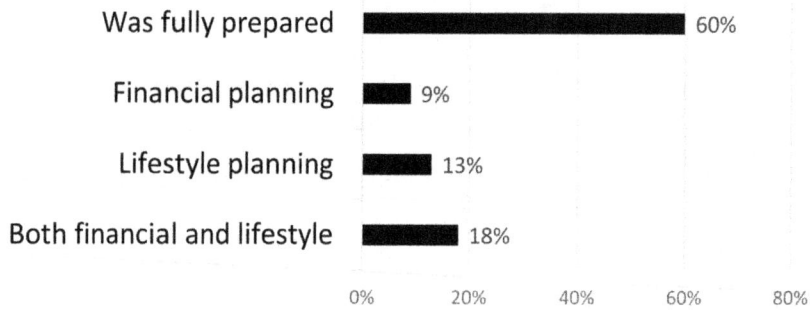

Was fully prepared — 60%

Financial planning — 9%

Lifestyle planning — 13%

Both financial and lifestyle — 18%

0%   20%   40%   60%   80%

Chart 5-3. Planning and Satisfaction

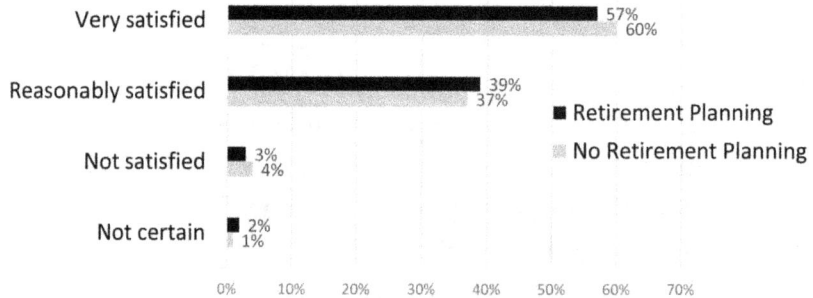

Very satisfied — 57% / 60%

Reasonably satisfied — 39% / 37%

Not satisfied — 3% / 4%

Not certain — 2% / 1%

■ Retirement Planning

▨ No Retirement Planning

0%   10%   20%   30%   40%   50%   60%   70%

To explain this to the group, I said, "Let's change the focus and look at the connection between Life Goal and financial planning."

"But I'm already re-tired," said Les. "It's too late."

"I realize that," I acknowledged. "But the benefits of combining the two can apply any time before or after re-tirement, and they can apply to areas that may surprise you."

"But Dave and I have a financial planner," Diane added. "And he's done a pretty good job considering the ups and downs of the market."

"That's great," I said. "But tell me, when you started with him, how did he set up your plan? What I mean is, did he sit down with you to determine a financial goal for re-tirement?"

Dave looked at Diane with a quizzical expression and replied, "Yes, I think he did."

"Don't you remember," said Diane. "We spent a lot of time with him initially, and he asked us a bunch of questions to get an idea of our financial situation."

"How did you establish your financial goal?" I asked.

"I don't remember," said Dave.

"I do," replied Diane. "We told him we wanted to maximize our income and minimize our taxes. But I think he came up with a number based on a percentage of our income."

FINANCIAL AND LIFE GOAL

Establishing a financial goal is central to developing a financial plan – you have to know where you are heading before you can devise a plan to get there. The Financial Planning Association states, "The financial planning profession exists to help people reach their financial goals and dreams" (www.fpanet.org). As a non-financial planner observing the financial planning process, most financial planners claim to personalize financial planning. Still, few can 'walk the talk' because they do not have the tools to follow through. The problem is that most people don't have a clear idea of their 're-tirement dreams' or how they plan to spend their time in re-tirement, which is critical for establishing a financial goal. As I mentioned to Dave earlier, two-thirds of pre-re-tirees I meet in my workshops do not have concrete plans for re-tirement. So, they or their financial planners have to make an educated guess to identify their financial goals.

Most financial planners estimate a financial goal as somewhere between seventy and eighty percent of the individual's annual salary before re-tirement. This can present problems. First, many people may not have any idea what their future salary will be, and the further from re-tirement, the more problematic this becomes. Second, everybody is different. Some people may not need that much in re-tirement, while others may need more. If Dave started working with his son-in-law and earned extra income, he may not need as much as originally planned. If it didn't work out, he could need more. Third, financial conditions could change significantly before or after re-tirement, and the financial plan should be able to account for these differences. This is where Life Goal Planning can help.

"To understand how the two forms of planning interact and influence each other, we can look at planning a vacation. In planning a vacation, one of the most important things you must determine in advance is how much it will cost. To figure this out, you have to decide..." I wrote the words on a sheet of paper.

Figure 5-1

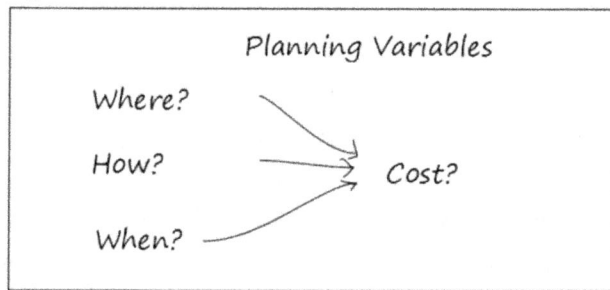

Planning Variables

Where?

How?   Cost?

When?

"Where you are going, how you will get there, and when you will leave. Now, let's suppose you know the where, how, and when of your vacation, and you determine the cost and decide that, given your current financial situation, it is too expensive. You can still take a vacation, provided you adjust some of the other variables. For example, you can go to a less expensive destination or find a less expensive hotel to adjust the where variable. To adjust the how variable, you can go on a camping trip or travel during low season to adjust the when variable. If these options are not acceptable or you don't want to make any changes, you can postpone your vacation to save more money until you can afford the vacation you want.

"Financial planning for re-tirement should involve the same variables and a similar process. So, before you establish your financial goal or calculate how much your re-tirement will cost, you have to determine the where, how, and when of re-tirement. Let's start with the first variable, where you are going. As we discussed, your objective or destination is to satisfy your needs and skills, especially those lost from work. You know how to identify these items, so you should be able to accurately identify your destination. Second, how will you get there? This includes the plans you have made to reach your destination. You have learned how to evaluate and perhaps improve on a plan and come up with new plans. If you include when you plan to re-tire and your risk level, you have the core information you need to develop a personalized plan to estimate your future financial needs or goals.

"Another way to look at this connection is that Life Goal and financial planning share the same objective. They both involve helping you plan for a life after work that will be worthwhile and enjoyable. The difference is that financial planning focuses on financing or funding a future lifestyle. In contrast, Life Goal Planning focuses on how to find a future lifestyle that will enable you to replace the satisfactions you have lost from work. The connection is in the keywords 'finance' and 'find'. Planning how to get there and making corrections starts by knowing where you are heading.

"Let's look at a different scenario. Suppose you re-tire or are re-tired, your financial situation changes, and you have a financial shortfall."

Les seemed to perk up at this point, so I explained, "Suppose you determine where, how, and when you will re-tire and discover that your financial situation will not support your intended re-tirement lifestyle. You have an imbalance with a financial shortfall. You know how you would like to spend your time in re-tirement but your financial situation won't support your plans. To continue with the vacation analogy, after you determine the where, how, and when of re-tirement and calculate the cost, if you decide you can't afford to re-tire, to correct this situation, if you look strictly for a financial solution, you can work longer, sell assets, or invest for a higher return. If you don't want to or can't adjust the financial domain, there is another option. You can adjust some - but not all - of the lifestyle variables. You can adjust the 'when' variable or postpone re-tirement or the 'how' variable and find re-tirement activities that satisfy the same needs but cost less. Remember, the key to re-tirement happiness is to satisfy your needs, and often you can satisfy the same need or skill through a different activity. The one variable that remains constant regardless of your financial circumstances is your 'where' variable - your Life Goal, or the needs and skills you hope to satisfy in re-tirement."

USE LATERAL THINKING

My concern with the issue is on a broader level, looking at how to satisfy your needs through different re-tirement plans that cost less. You can apply the Life Goal Planning techniques outlined in Chapter 3, only here you will be looking for activities that satisfy the items on your Life Goal List with the added condition or need that the suggested activities are less costly. An example might help here. Suppose you include travel as part of your re-tirement plans but realize now that you cannot afford it. Start by identifying your needs that will be met through this activity. Look at your Life Goal List, select another column, identify those items you will meet through travel, and then brainstorm an alternative, alone or with others, that could satisfy those needs and the additional need of costing less.

Broaden your thinking and remember that you can often meet the same need through a different activity. So, besides thinking about ways to travel more economically, for example, driving instead of flying, renting a mobile home instead of a condo, or a home swap for an extended stay, try to come up with some creative alternatives. I know a lawyer who re-tired and became a travel writer for a local publication. He wasn't paid for his writing, but he and his wife have taken advantage of free travel provided by various hotels, restaurants, and cruise lines. Try to stretch your imagination and be creative. Maybe you can find a non-travel, less expensive alternative that satisfies many of the same needs. Life Goal Planning can be your ace in the hole. You have the tools to adjust the lifestyle dimension, and you do not have to rely solely on the financial dimension for your re-tirement happiness.

VOLUNTEERING

To change the subject, I asked them if they were involved with voluntary or charitable organizations. Janice mentioned being part of an adult literacy program and told us the benefits of her volunteer work.

Les then said, "Janice keeps telling me that I should join the program, but the truth is, I am just not interested. I feel a bit guilty about that, especially since I have so much free time on my hands."

I asked Dave and Diane if they had ever been involved in volunteer work, and they said they had not. Then I said, "When we did our survey among re-tirees, 51% mentioned that they pursued some type of volunteer or charitable activity. It's often looked on as the ideal re-tirement activity that could replace satisfactions lost from work without the constraints of a paid job and can be viewed as a win-win situation, with the added benefit of giving back to society and benefiting the recipients."

In response to Les's comments about feeling guilty, I wanted to clarify a few issues and said, "We found a curious situation among the people in our survey who volunteered. When we asked if they volunteered before they re-tired, 88% were involved with these types of activities before re-tirement, and 88% of the charitable activities they pursued before re-tirement were mostly the same as those pursued in re-tirement. This suggests that people who were inclined to volunteer in re-tirement were also more likely to pursue these activities before they re-tired. In other words, volunteering is not for everyone, and if you are not so inclined, you need not feel guilty."

"Well, I suppose you are right," replied Les, "but I still wish I could find something to fill my time."

"Another issue to think about," I said, "is to be aware of the possibility of rejection even in a volunteer situation." It told them about George, from my workshop, who sold his business. Thinking about what he could do in re-tirement, he discovered a government agency that paired re-tired business people with young entrepreneurs. He had developed a very successful business and was excited about sharing his 'street smarts'. By the way, he had never volunteered before. When he contacted the agency, he was told they had too many re-tired business people and not enough interested entrepreneurs. Although this was not a personal rejection, he was essentially told that he was not needed. George felt rejected and deflated. Nevertheless, and this is hypothetical, he could have learned something from this experience. For example, after learning that the agency did not have enough entrepreneurs signed up, he could have approached the agency and volunteered to find entrepreneurs; he still had many business contacts from the past. On the other hand, he could have talked to others who felt like him, and together they may be able to develop some alternative method to help others. Once the creative juices begin to flow, opportunities are endless.

RE-TIREMENT MENTORS AND VOLUNTEERING

Chart 5-4 includes the types of volunteer activities pursued by your re-tirement mentors.

Chart 5-4. Voluntary Pursuits

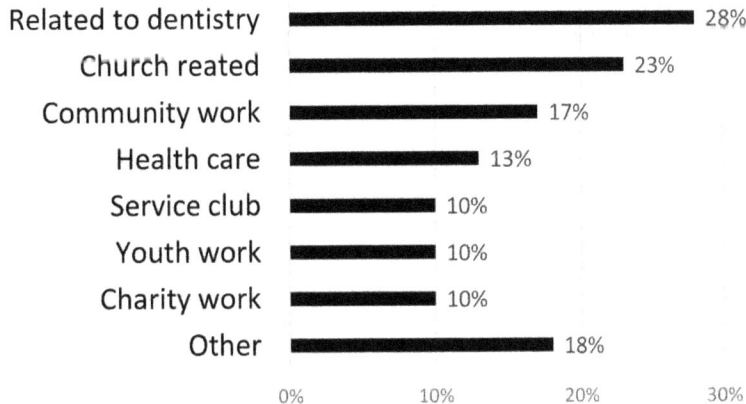

Activity	Percentage
Related to dentistry	28%
Church reated	23%
Community work	17%
Health care	13%
Service club	10%
Youth work	10%
Charity work	10%
Other	18%

Two points stand out. First, one benefit of dentistry, compared to most other professions, is the opportunity to continue involvement in dentistry after re-tirement - both locally and abroad. Here are a few examples.

2 days dental treatment provider at Free Clinic.

Dental mission trips to Puerto Rico.

Dentistry for folks with challenges.

Free dentistry and Mission of Mercy.

Free dental clinic with my instruments and former assistant. Mentoring clinical senior dental students, until I did not renew my license. Big mistake on my part.

Traveled to foreign country with Medical/Dental team and served on various dental committees, councils.

US Navy Pacific Partnership missions aboard hospital ships. Missions to Indonesia, Philippines, Samoa and Tonga..

Volunteer dentistry in Nicaragua, Honduras, Dominican Republic, Peru, Ecuador, etc. Just returned from Borneo where I distributed 400 toothbrushes at a Catholic orphanage. LOTS of volunteer work!

Another observation is the high percentage of activities designated as 'Other' volunteer opportunities - those beyond what most people expect from volunteer opportunities. For example,

Assist in a fitness program for Parkinson afflicted participants

Bee keeping mentor

Hobby is woodturning- I serve as mentor to young men who seek their way in life and I donate works of art for various charities

Humane society

Library board, conservation authority

Love music. Have been a DJ at a public radio station

Music program for disadvantage/ low income children.

On board of Chamber Orchestra

Raise money for music scholarship.

Refugee resettlement

Renovations for seniors and work at animal shelters

Treasurer and director of Search and Rescue

Volunteer at public library delivering books to homebound clients

Volunteer for a horseback riding therapy group for handicapped persons, River Water

Volunteered in state election campaign of local dentist running for House

Working with non-kill animal shelter for dogs and cats.

When re-tirement satisfaction was related to volunteering, we did not detect any significant difference between those who did, and those who is not volunteer in re-tirement.

Chart 5-5. Volunteering and Satisfaction

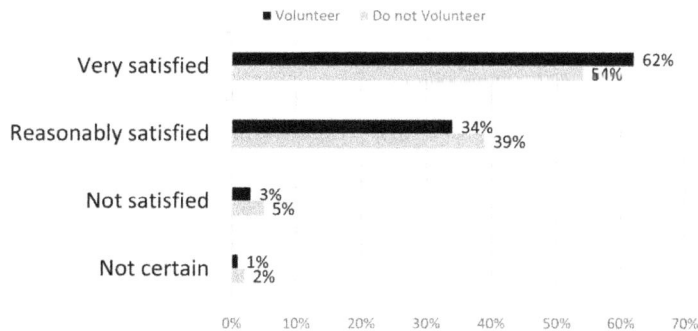

■ Volunteer   ▨ Do not Volunteer

Very satisfied	62% / 51%
Reasonably satisfied	34% / 39%
Not satisfied	3% / 5%
Not certain	1% / 2%

0%   10%   20%   30%   40%   50%   60%   70%

There are many volunteer opportunities beyond the traditional healthcare situations, and there are many websites devoted to matching volunteers with agencies. A cursory look at one site included an art and wine reception coordinator, web site designers, grant writers, theatrical groups, media and communication internships, and the list goes on.

CHAPTER SUMMARY

- You have two re-tirement goals, a 'Financial Goal' and a 'Life Goal' and each requires different planning methods. Your financial goal is to finance your re-tirement, and your Life Goal is to satisfy your personal needs in re-tirement. The link between these goals lies in the type of activities you pursue; you want to find activities that will satisfy your needs and that you can afford.

- Planning for re-tirement starts by having some idea of how much it will cost - a financial goal. First you have to identify the needs and skills you want to satisfy in re-tirement (your re-tirement Life Goal), and the activities you plan to pursue to satisfy your re-tirement Life Goal. Then if you factor in your re-tirement date, you can develop a personalized financial plan.

- If you have a financial shortfall at re-tirement, besides considering changes in the financial domain, Life Goal Planning will enable you to create alternative and possibly less costly activities in the non-financial domain that will satisfy your needs lost from work.

- The Life Goal Planning Exercises in Part 2, include a section to summarize your findings that can be shared with a financial planner to incorporate with your financial plan.

- Volunteering can be viewed as a win-win situation that can replace many satisfactions formerly met by work with the added benefit of giving back to society.

- 51% of your re-tirement mentors pursued volunteer activities and only 28% of the volunteer activities related directly to dentistry.

- 84% were involved with these types of activities before re-tirement, and 88% of the volunteer activities in re-tirement were mostly or somewhat the same as those pursed before they re-tired. This suggests that those people who were inclined to volunteer in re-tirement were more likely to pursue these activities before they re-tired.

- Volunteering is not for everyone and if you are not so inclined, you need not feel guilty.

Chapter 6

DID YOU EVER HAVE TO
MAKE UP YOUR MIND?
(The Lovin'Spoonfull, 1965)

The Decision to Re-tire

Every summer, the people who live in our neighborhood get together for a block party. It's an informal potluck affair, and various families contribute drinks and food. This tradition has been going on for several years and always includes a collection of adults, kids, and dogs. I often see people I have not seen since last summer's party. This year, the party took place a few weeks after my session with Dave and Diane, and I was curious to see if they continued with the program on their own and if it was helping Dave with his re-tirement plans.

When we arrived at the party, I waved at Dave and Diane, who were speaking to a few other people. My wife spotted and joined an old friend. Diane signaled for me to join them, and as I approached, I heard him say, "Here's the guy I was telling you about. I'll introduce you."

Dave introduced me to Lynn, who recently moved into the neighborhood. He explained that they were talking about the session at his house a few weeks ago. He also introduced Craig, who was re-tired.

After the introductions, Lynn said, "Dave tells me that you help people plan for re-tirement."

"Well, yes," I replied. "I conduct workshops and focus on the non-financial side of re-tirement."

Dave interjected and said, "We have been talking about re-tirement, and

I told them about your new way of looking at re-tirement, with a dash. It's funny, but lately I have spoken to quite a few people who are starting to think about it."

"Let's face it," I said. "Re-tirement is becoming a fact of life for people our age. Suddenly it's no longer far off in the future. Now, it's a reality."

I asked Craig what he did before he re-tired. He said he was in the insurance business and re-tired a few years ago.

"Well," I asked, "how is re-tirement treating you?"

"It's great," he replied.

"He's a politician," said Diane. "Don't you recognize him? He's a city politician."

"I knew your name sounded familiar," I said. "How did you get into politics?"

"I have been interested in politics for many years, and I like to be involved. When I re-tired, I thought, what the heck, why not go for it? I love the job, actually."

Lynn had a thoughtful look and said, "If I had a million dollars in the bank, I'd re-tire tomorrow."

I had come across this type of thinking before, so I told Lynn, "I once met a guy who said the same thing. I think he was willing to re-tire for less, but that was some time ago, and with inflation today, he may say one million. The point is, I got the impression that his thoughts on re-tiring ran much deeper than an amount of money in the bank."

To expand on this issue, I said, "Let me ask you a couple of questions, Lynn. Suppose you had a million dollars in the bank."

"That would be nice," she replied.

"Would you re-tire?"

She considered her answer, and with a slight grin on her face, she said, "I really don't know."

"Fair enough," I said. "The next question is, if you had a million dollars in the bank and after meeting me, would you say to me, if only I had two million dollars in the bank, I would re-tire tomorrow?"

She smiled and said, "That's a good question. The truth is, I have a love/

hate thing with my job, and re-tirement may be an option."

"When can you re-tire?" I asked.

"I'm a lawyer, and with my firm I can re-tire whenever I want. Some people in our firm should have re-tired years ago, and maybe I am one of them. Nevertheless, I'm still hanging in and plodding away. For me, it's a tough decision to make. What happens if I don't like it?"

Lynn asked me at what age most people re-tire, and I told her there is no simple answer to that question. Statistically people are re-tiring younger, but statistics mean nothing. Everybody's conditions are different. "For some people, the decision is made for them by the rules set out in their pension formula or the workplace, although mandatory re-tirement is fast becoming a thing of the past, or by health considerations. For people who have some control over when they can re-tire, it can be a difficult decision because so many factors can come into play.

I asked Lynn if she had any plans for re-tirement.

"The problem is," she replied, "I could re-tire, but I like my work. I mean, it has its problems, but I like going to work."

"Then why are you thinking about re-tiring?" I asked. "If you don't have to re-tire and if you enjoy your work, there is nothing wrong with staying where you are."

"I realize that," said Lynn. "But a few of my friends have re-tired, and I guess it's kind of infectious. One of my closest friends re-tired last year, and she is having a great time. I hardly get a chance to see her anymore. And look at Craig; he's having the time of his life."

Craig beamed in agreement, so I asked him how he decided to re-tire.

"I can't remember, exactly," he replied. "But as I said, I have always been interested in politics, and quite frankly, I have been in insurance for so long that I needed a change. So, it came naturally. One day, I sat down and asked myself, if not now, when? I guess I am lucky. In a way, the decision was not hard to make."

I turned to Lynn and said, "Lynn, to get back to your comment about having enough money to re-tire, I have spoken to many people in a similar situation. A few weeks ago, Dave and I talked about this issue. If you are thinking about when to re-tire, I can't decide for you, but I can give you some things to think about."

"I would appreciate that," said Lynn.

We sat down, and I said, "Let's put re-tirement aside for a moment. Say you had another decision to make, such as you want to buy a new car. How would you decide on which car was best for you?"

"I would test-drive a few cars to see which one I preferred," said Dave.

"Suppose you still couldn't decide after a test drive. What else could you do to help with this decision?"

"You could read consumer reports," said Lynn. "Or talk to people who owned each car to get their impressions. Also, you could look at the resale values and safety reports."

"In other words," I said, "you should do your homework. You should gather, compare, and weigh the relevant information. You can apply the same process of gathering, comparing, and weighing the relevant information to the decision to re-tire.

"The first step," I said, "is to do your homework. You have to gather the relevant information and look at the various factors that can bear on this decision."

I addressed all of them and asked, "What information should you gather in deciding to re-tire. What factors can come into play?"

Lynn said, "Let me think. I haven't thought about this before. I suppose health can be important. If you are having health problems, you might want to re-tire. And, of course, money is important."

"Yes, money and health can influence the decision to re-tire," I replied. "But can you think of anything else?"

"If you didn't like your work, you might be anxious to re-tire," said Craig.

"That can be very important," I said. "We could also include family considerations and the timing of a spouse's re-tirement. These can influence the decisions of some people. There are three main factors to consider in the decision to re-tire. Other factors include health, the timing of a spouse's re-tirement, and so on."

PUSH AND PULL FACTORS

I looked around for something to write on, reached for a napkin, and wrote the following:

$$\$$$

Push

Pull

"He loves to write messages," said Dave. "The other day, he kept writing messages on his fence."

I let this comment pass, smiled, and said, "To make a rational decision about when to re-tire, you have to gather information on these three factors. Push factors include the things you are happy to give up at work, Pull factors are the things you look forward to in re-tirement, and money is money.

"Let's start with money because the first thing that pops into most people's minds when they think of when to re-tire is whether they will have enough money to re-tire. As you said, Lynn, if only you had a million dollars, you would re-tire tomorrow."

"I was just joking," she replied.

"Well," I said, "most people think this way, and money is an important consideration. When most people think about re-tirement planning, the first and often the only thing they think about is financial planning."

"That's true," said Lynn. "When I thought about re-tiring, I only thought about how much I needed to re-tire."

"Having enough money is both a quantitative and qualitative judgment," I explained. "The distinction here is between money expressed as a dollar figure, such as I need X dollars to re-tire. Of course, the problem is if you don't know how you will spend your time in re-tirement, it can be difficult to figure out if you have enough money.

"The other problem is that 'need' is a qualitative entity, and only you can judge when enough is enough. So, in the context of deciding to re-tire, besides looking at how much money you need, the quantitative dimension, you also have to ask yourself:

When does the fun begin?"

"Does this question sound familiar?" I asked.

"It sure does," said Craig. "Would you believe that I used to have a T-shirt with that written on it?"

"And I recall seeing bumper stickers with this question," I replied.

"Your answer to this question is the first step in the qualitative approach to the decision to re-tire. Would you agree that the word fun is another way of saying enjoyment? I asked"

"Sure," said Lynn. "They mean the same thing."

"As I outlined to Dave and Diane a few weeks ago, we enjoy any activity before or after re-tirement because it satisfies our needs. For example, suppose you think about why you may be enjoying this block party. In that case, you might say it satisfies your need to be in the sunshine, to relax, to meet people, eat potato salad, and as an added surprise bonus, to learn something about re-tirement."

"Sounds reasonable," said Lynn. "But what does a party have to do with re-tirement?"

"They are similar because both will be enjoyable if they satisfy your needs. Therefore, the question 'When will the fun begin?' becomes..." I reached for another napkin.

When can I
satisfy my
needs?

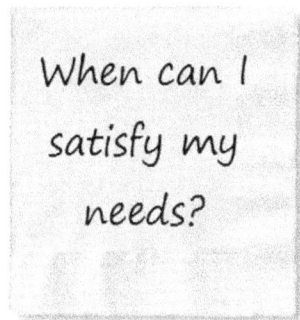

"In fact, because of the freedom of re-tirement, it can be the perfect opportunity to satisfy your needs."

"It all sounds good," said Lynn, "but I like some parts of my work, and I am not so sure about this."

Dave agreed with Lynn on this point.

"The main thing I am suggesting is that in thinking about re-tiring, keep this question in mind," I pointed to my napkin, "as I mentioned before, money alone will not guarantee re-tirement happiness. And some people may use the excuse of not having enough money, where the real problem is they don't know how to replace satisfactions lost from work."

I looked back at my first napkin and said, "The next thing to consider is your Push Factors. Push factors include everything you would be happy to give up or leave behind when you re-tire. These are, figuratively speaking, pushing you into re-tirement. The Pull considerations include the things you are looking forward to in re-tirement, which pull you into re-tirement.

"Here is what I suggest you do. Start by listing your Push and Pull considerations on a piece of paper. Give this some serious thought, and don't be too hasty. Then, take a hard look at the items in both categories. After comparing your Push and Pull factors, it may become clear which option is the best. It would be preferable if you based your decision mainly on Pull factors. If not, re-tiring may be a case of going from the frying pan into the fire. Eventually, everyone has to re-tire, so you had better get to work to redress the balance between your Push and Pull considerations. If you looked forward to re-tirement, you would base your decision mainly on pull factors."

"That sounds like a worthwhile exercise. I will try it," said Lynn.

"Just use this simple formula."

$$NR >= NW$$
$$NW >= NR$$

"What does that stand for?" Diane asked.

"It's a shorthand formula," I replied. "NR stands for needs in re-tirement, and NW stands for needs at work. So it reads, you should consider re-tiring when your needs met in re-tirement will be greater than or equal to those currently met at work."

Dave studied my formula and said, "Sounds a bit formal, but that's an interesting way to look at it. How can I figure this out?"

I explained to the others that I taught Dave and Diane some of the basics of Life Goal Planning a few weeks ago and based my explanation on that process.

"It's very simple," I replied, "and you're halfway there. When you evaluated your re-tirement plans to see if they would meet your needs and skills, although we only included a few questions, you should have a pretty good idea of those needs and skills that will be met when you re-tire. That takes care of the left side of this equation. Now, all you have to do is use another column in your Life Goal sheet to evaluate the needs and skills you have met at work and then compare the two columns.

"Now I get it," said Dave."

"So let me ask you again, Lynn. If you had a million dollars in the bank, would you re-tire tomorrow?"

Lynn smiled and said, "Not until my Pull factors outweighed my Push factors."

DECISION TO RE-TIRE

Eighty-one percent of your re-tirement mentors indicated that they re-tired by choice, with a slight gender difference (M = 82%, F = 70%). Their reasons for re-tiring on Chart 6-1, included both Pull Factors (things they looked forward to in re-tirement), and Push Factors (things they were quite happy to give up from work). Note that the females were more likely to be unhappy with their work situation and to re-tire for health reasons.

Chart 6-1. Reason for Re-tiring
■ Male   ▨ Female

Reason	Male	Female
Felt it was time to retire	63%	45%
To do other things	46%	39%
Retirement income was sufficient	50%	34%
More time for self/family	47%	57%
Problems with practice/dentistry	14%	34%
Health reasons	19%	34%
Spouse retired then	8%	11%

Here are a few 'Other' reasons for re-tiring.

Changed career to primarily teaching.

I found out a respected colleague of mine helped dentists in transition, I respected him so much I merely asked him if he felt I would able to and if anyone may be interested in purchasing my practice? Several months later, after he had found several interested dentists, things came together so rapidly that I was surprised, thankful, and made the decision with my dear wife who had been my loyal assistant for 30 years, to actually make our decision and follow through with the opportunity!

I found the right guy to take over the practice and it was a one time opportunity.

My work load seemed light enough to condense it from four to three days per week. It was an experiment that worked out well.

Spouse died and I lost my desire to continue practicing.

The delayed financial fallout from the 2009-2010 recession resulted in a lower patient load. I reduced my days in the office per week by one, and discovered that I liked it, and it was financially sustainable.

The practice selling price was at or near the peak and the future projections were going down.

The right young orthodontist came along and I did want to get involved with my family in a winery.

Too many new rules/regulations to deal with. I had three employees and did all the paperwork myself.

Wanted to realize the value of the practice. Sold at peak. Wanted smooth transition for patients and staff. Allow new owners to purchase/invest in major new technology. Wanted practice to continue smoothly in case unexpected health issues arose. Concentrate on the things I love about dentistry, and let someone else do the things I didn't like. Have more flexibility and freedom.

To see the relationship between age and re-tirement, Chart 6-2 indicates that the females in our sample tended to re-tire younger than the males. Chart 6-3 includes responses to the question, "If you could do it over again would you still retire at the same age?". In this case the men were more likely to re-tire at the same age, while a much higher percentage of women were 'not certain' about this issue.

Chart 6-2. Age at Re-tirement

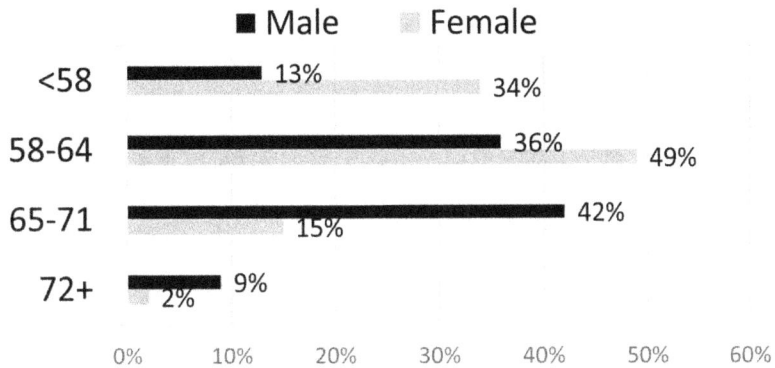

■ Male   ▨ Female

Age	Male	Female
<58	13%	34%
58-64	36%	49%
65-71	42%	15%
72+	9%	2%

Chart 6-3. Re-tire at the Same Age

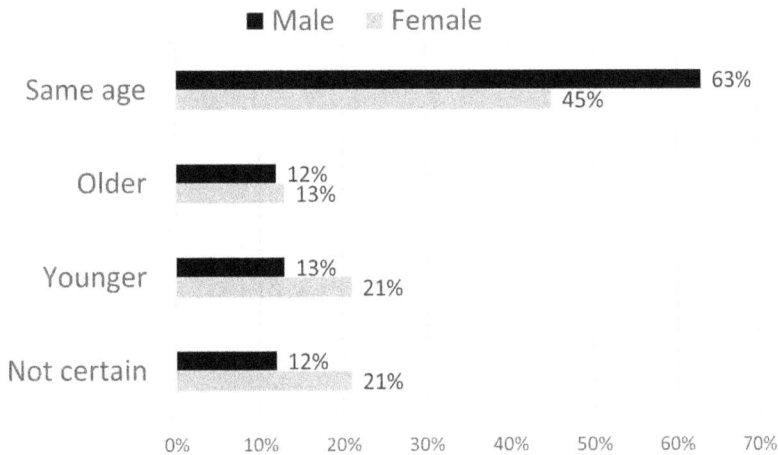

■ Male   ▨ Female

	Male	Female
Same age	63%	45%
Older	12%	13%
Younger	13%	21%
Not certain	12%	21%

SPOUSES RE-TIRING TOGETHER

"One thing we have been thinking about," said Dave, "is if Diane and I should re-tire at the same time."

"This can complicate things," I said.

I turned to Lynn and Craig and asked them if this was a concern. Lynn said that she was a single mother and that it was not an issue for her, but she was interested to hear what I had to say about it. Craig said that his wife was still working.

I turned back to Dave and Diane and said, "Some couples prefer to re-tire at the same time, while others do not. This decision involves several factors that deserve serious consideration. From a purely financial perspective, it might reduce her pension if Diane takes an early re-tirement."

"That is not a major problem for us," said Dave.

I told them about a couple from one of my workshops who faced this decision. I met Cindy when she was about to re-tire from her job. But she was not looking forward to it because she did not want to spend time with her retired (without the dash) husband. It seems that several years ago, Cindy and her husband both retired simultaneously. They had not discussed this in detail, but she retired from her job early to spend time with her husband. The way Cindy described her situation, the day after her husband retired, he reached into his job jar and decided to paint the house. He woke up at his usual time, and they had breakfast together. Then he went outside to paint the house. At 10:00, he took a break and had coffee together. Then he went back to painting the house. At noon they had lunch together, 2:30 he took a coffee break, and at 4:30, he quit working.

The next day, he followed the same routine until he finally finished painting the house. At that point, Cindy thought, "Great, now we can spend some time together." Well, it didn't work out that way. After painting the house, he rebuilt the garden, and when he ran out of jobs to do at home, he volunteered to help their neighbors fix up their places. Eventually, he ran out of jobs to do.

Then, the real trouble began. He started watching TV in the afternoon and hanging around shopping centers because he had nothing to do. Cindy was so frustrated that she returned to her former employer and begged to get her job back. Her former boss rehired her a few years ago, and now she was coming up to mandatory retirement and was not looking forward to it.

After relating Cindy and her husband's story, I did not want them to think this was common. So I said, "This is a rather extreme case, and I am not suggesting that it has anything to do with you and Diane. However, it touches on several points that are worth thinking about.

"The first point is the decision for a couple to re-tire together should not be taken for granted. It requires honest, open dialogue well in advance of re-tirement. Cindy and her husband had completely different expectations about how they would spend their re-tirement. She expected to spend time with her husband while he had other ideas. It is also clear that they did not express their feelings about re-tirement before they re-tired. If they had spent time before re-tirement talking about what each thought they would like to do, and if her husband had been honest, as a minimum, Cindy would not have taken an early re-tirement.

"The next consideration is that it appears that Cindy and her husband failed to find worthwhile alternatives after retirement (retired without the dash). Her husband seemingly had plenty to do that he enjoyed when he retired. Nevertheless, eventually, he ran out of things to keep himself busy.

"Cindy, on the other hand, did not have any re-tirement plans and was relying on her husband so they could do things together. Unfortunately, when this failed to materialize, her only consideration was to return to work (she took the easy way out). Like her husband, she had nothing worthwhile to sustain herself in retirement."

Cindy's husband reminded me of people who, soon after re-tirement say they have so much to do that there aren't enough hours in the day to do it all. For some people, this may be true. Others, I suspect, are filling time with 'busy work.' They lack a Central Life Focus in re-tirement. In addition, when they run out of busy work, problems can set in.

I turned to Dave and Diane and said, "Now is the time for you to start talking about various scenarios for when either or both of you re-tire. Diane, are you considering early re-tirement if Dave re-tires soon?"

"I'm not sure what to do," she replied. "We have talked about this, but we haven't decided yet. We like to do things together, but this is a major decision. If Dave returns to work, I might as well stay at work. If he doesn't, then maybe I will re-tire. It depends."

"Here's what I suggest you do," I said. "Both of you should complete the two exercises I mentioned earlier. Evaluate your re-tirement plans and current work based on your needs and skills. We did this with your re-tirement plans at your house a few weeks ago. This should identify any problems or omissions in either or both of your plans before you re-tire, then you can compare re-tirement with your current work.

"Then think about and list your Push and Pull considerations. If your Push outweighs your Pull list, think about reversing this situation. Think about creating a re-tirement that would be preferable to being at work. Do these exercises in the context of the broader question, 'When does the fun begin?' If you are honest with yourselves and spend some time with this, the answer you have been searching for might appear."

"After the session at our house," said Diane, "we both have been looking at our plans. Now we will try these other exercises."

There was a slight pause, and Dave said, "There is one more thing that has been bothering me. I hate to admit it, but when I think about re-tiring, it's as if I'm getting old. Do you know what I mean? I don't want people to think of me as a senior citizen. It scares me."

"I feel the same way Dave," said Lynn. "I know it's silly, but you can't deny some things."

"You are touching on an important topic near and dear to my heart," I replied. "I say this because I have spent many years teaching re-tirement education, and although this concern is common, it is completely misplaced. The problem is if you believe that re-tirement is somehow connected to aging or growing old, and this is a common belief, it can have negative consequences. I am not denying that we are getting older. I am simply stating that aging has absolutely nothing to do with re-tirement. The problem is that most people, including many who write books and run courses on retirement, do not understand this issue. Before we get into that subject, one of my immediate needs is to get more delicious potato salad. After I satisfy this need, I will show you a completely different way to look at the issue of aging and re-tirement. I am not trying to sweep this under the carpet, hoping it will disappear or not be noticed. I want to show you that your concern about growing old and re-tirement is unwarranted and harmful. I'll be right back."

CHAPTER SUMMARY

- Money alone will not guarantee re-tirement happiness and some people use the excuse of not having enough money, where the real problem is they don't know how to replace satisfactions lost from work.

- To make a rational decision about when to re-tire, you have to gather information on three factors: push factors (the things you are happy to give up at work), pull factors, (the things you look forward to in re-tirement), and money.

- List and compare your Push and Pull considerations. If your financial situation is adequate, you should consider re-tiring when the needs you expect to meet in re-tirement will be greater than or equal to those currently met at work.

- The decision for a couple to re-tire together requires honest, open dialogue well in advance of re-tirement.

- Eighty-one percent of your re-tirement mentors re-tired by choice, and their top 5 reasons included; felt it was time to re-tire, to do things besides work, re-tirement income was sufficient, to spend more time with self or family, and problems with dentistry or their practice.

Chapter 7

WHEN I'M SIXTY-FOUR
(The Beatles, 1967)

Aging and Re-tirement

I have spent over 30 years studying, researching, writing about, and teaching the re-tirement experience. This includes many years teaching Social Gerontology (the study of aging) during my university experience and working with thousands of pre- and post-re-trees through my workshops. Based on this experience, I have concluded that in the context of re-tirement, a discussion on aging is irrelevant and detrimental. It is irrelevant because aging has nothing to do with re-tirement, and it is detrimental because it can reinforce the commonly held misconception that when one re-tires, one is getting old. This may have applied to generations of retirees in the past, but it most certainly does not apply today, especially with people re-tiring so young. So pervasive is the issue that I felt compelled to clear up a few misconceptions.

I returned with a bowl of potato salad, sat down, and said, "When we talked about re-tirement and aging, you said you were concerned about people thinking of you as old. Unfortunately, this feeling is common and tied into the traditional image of retirement (without the dash) I discussed earlier with Dave. The problem is that most people, including many who write books and run courses on retirement, make this connection. They make the connection because it has always been part of the thinking about retirement (without the dash), and coincidentally, we tend to be older when we re-tire."

AGING AND THE SELF-FULFILLING PROPHECY

The aging process begins at birth. It is common, however, to use the term aging to refer to growing older. It is also common to make the connection between aging in the context of growing older and re-tirement. In fact, one dictionary defines retirement as "to withdraw from office, business, or active life, usually because of age (dictionary.com). The structure of private and public pension schemes reinforces this connection. Typically, people re-tire when they are eligible to receive a full pension, and the timing is according to age (or some formula taking into account years of service and age). Rather than performance, age is the determining factor because of convenience and tradition. To my mind, it is wrong to base the point of re-tirement primarily on age. Having said that, if we must use age to expedite re-tirement and calculate pension rates, we must not assume a relation between re-tirement and aging or getting old. If you believe this, you are guilty of what I call the 'ageist's self-fulfilling prophecy'. The heart of the matter is wrapped up in the self-fulfilling prophecy concept."

Initially conceptualized by Robert Merton in the 1950s, the self-fulfilling prophecy occurs when a false definition of the situation evokes a new behavior, which makes the original false conception come true. In plain English, if we believe something strongly, even if it isn't accurate, we tend to act in ways consistent with that expectation. Chapter 1 included an example of the salesman and the missing jack.

Here is another example from Groucho Marx, the comedian, through a transcript from a recently rediscovered radio show aired in 1933. Groucho Marx, Attorney at Law, is speaking to his secretary about mailing a letter.

It's just a note to my friend, Steve Granach, asking for a loan...but he's probably got his own troubles. I hardly think he can spare it. And even if he had it, I think he'd be a little reluctant to lend me the dough. He's kind of tight that way. Why, I don't think he'd let me have it if I was going hungry. In fact, that guy wouldn't give me a nickel if I were starving. And he calls himself a friend...the cheap swine. I'll show him where to get off. Take a letter to that snake and tell him I wouldn't touch his money. And if he ever comes near this office again, I'll break every bone in his body.

In this example, Groucho defined the situation as one where even if his friend delivered the money personally, he still wouldn't take it. He would break every bone in his body! The self-fulfilling prophecy closely relates to the definition of the situation described earlier. The salesman in Chapter 1 and Groucho Marx defined their situations (needing a jack and asking for a loan), so they no longer wanted the jack or the loan.

After briefly describing the self-fulfilling prophecy to the group, I said, "The same situation can occur concerning aging and re-tirement. For example, in my workshop, I met someone who believed he would not live very long after he re-tired. This was extreme thinking, and obviously, I was quite surprised to hear him say this, so I asked how long his parents lived. His mother was 82 and was still alive. His father lived to be over 80. There was no biological reason for his belief. But the problem was, he so firmly held on to this belief that he may help to bring it about."

AGEIST SELF-FULFILLING PROPHECY

I explained that this man was guilty of the Ageist Self-fulfilling Prophecy. An ageist is to older people as a racist is to certain ethnic groups, and a sexist is to women. Ageism implies prejudice or discrimination against or negative attitudes toward people based on their age. For our purposes, the Ageist Self-fulfilling Prophecy means that if you believe that when you re-tire you will be old or that others will think of you that way, you may look for signs to validate your belief, and if you look hard enough, you will find them even if you must create them.

To give an example they could relate to, I asked, "Do any of you know of someone who passed away soon after re-tirement?"

A solemn hush fell over the group. This is a serious matter. After all, these people are about to re-tire, and the implications behind this thought are scary.

Diane said to Dave, "What about Alex? Didn't he die about a year after he re-tired?"

"Yes, he did," Dave replied, somewhat reluctantly. "And he wasn't that much older than me. It makes you wonder."

With a somber face, I replied, "Terrible isn't it?" I paused to let this thought sink in. Then I said, "Now let me ask, does anyone know someone who recently re-tired and is still alive?"

It took a few seconds for this thought to register, and when it did, the tone changed to laughter and relief.

"Our mind does funny things. This sticks in our mind if we hear of someone who dies soon after re-tirement. We think re-tirement killed them. However, we don't think about the millions of people who may live longer because they re-tired. In addition, there is no way to test if Alex would still be alive if he did not re-tire. Once somebody re-tires and dies, you can't bring them back to see if they would live longer by not re-tiring. Yet if we hear about someone dying soon after re-tirement, the ageist self-fulfilling prophecy leads us to believe that re-tirement was the cause."

INTERPRETING STATISTICS

I have come across several statements that have this effect. For example, "those who make no plans for their retirement years receive on average just 13 Social Security benefit checks, and seven out of 10 of them die within two years.[1] My response to these statistics can be summarized in a single word; "Hogwash." If we were to look deeper, the only way to determine if the statement is true that people who had no plans for retirement died within two years of retirement would be to ask them if they had plans. The problem is, they will have passed, so we can't ask them. Furthermore, if 70% die within two years, how can we prove that the 30% who live beyond two years of retirement made plans? Finally, having plans means nothing. The quality of those plans is what counts. Of course, the research did not report this. Be careful interpreting statistics.

MEMORY AND AGING

Another common example of the Ageist's Self-Fulfilling Prophecy is memory loss. To emphasize this, I said, "I have to admit that I know of a sign of aging that most people experience. Let me ask you another question. Do you find that as you get older, and I am not denying that we are getting older, you are starting to forget things, like people's names or where you left your keys?"

"Would you repeat the question," said Craig. "I forget what you were asking."

They all laughed at his comment, but I suspect deep down it was a nervous laugh and that they could relate to this problem.

To respond to Craig, I started repeating my question, stopped, and said, "Seriously, if you find that you are starting to forget things, is it logical to conclude that you are getting old?"

There was silence, so I said, "I have some good and bad news. The bad news is that if you believe that forgetting things is a sign of your age, you are a victim of the Ageist Self-fulfilling Prophecy. The good news is that forgetting things as you get older is not necessarily a result of your age."

"What else could it be?" asked Lynn.

"I will explain that in a minute," I replied.

"I admit that as people get older, there is one important thing they start to forget. I am not talking about forgetting where you put your car keys or a person's name. These are minor compared to what I am referring to."

I asked, "Can anybody tell me the most significant thing people forget as they get older?"

There was a pause, and then Diane said jokingly, "I can think of plenty of things, but I don't think Dave wants it aired in public."

"I think forgetting a person's name is pretty significant," said Lynn.

"It's only significant if you see it as a sign of aging," I said. "Besides, not everyone starts to forget people's names as they get older, and, in a moment, I will show you that it is not necessarily a sign of aging."

Again, I asked them what people forget as they get older, and because I did not receive an answer, I said, "The most important thing that people forget as they get older is that they used to forget things when they were younger."

I paused to let this sink in.

"And more importantly," I continued, "when you were 22 and forgot something, you never construed that as a sign of being young. You probably thought I had too much on my mind, or I will think of it eventually, or I should work at remembering those things, or you just accepted that you had a bad memory.

"But now, when you forget things, you interpret it as a sign of aging. Secretly, at the back of your mind, you think, oh my God, I must be getting senile or have Alzheimer's disease.

"This is the natural conclusion of false logic (or a false definition of the situation). If you start with the assumption that older people forget things and that re-tirees are old, and you start to forget things, the logical conclusion is that I must be getting old. You define the situation as real; look for clues to confirm it - like forgetting something - and it becomes real in its consequence. You reinforce the connection between re-tirement and growing old."

To elaborate on this sensitive issue, I told them about research on memory and aging, which generally supports the assumption that as people grow older, their short-term memory diminishes.

"The problem is," I said, "most of this research is based on the Ageist Self-fulfilling Prophecy. To explain what I mean, I can describe a piece of research I designed to look at the effects of height on short-term memory. I believe that short people have better short-term memory than tall people."

They looked surprised by this assertion, so I said, "Before jumping to any conclusions about my sanity, I am using a tongue-in-cheek example to make a point.

"To test my hypothesis that short people have better short-term memory than tall people, suppose I asked everyone at this street party to line up from the shortest to the tallest, and then I divided them into two groups based on their height. Then, I would give each person a short-term memory test to recall several objects after a 15-minute interval.

"Now let's suppose that, on average, the short people did marginally better than the tall people in recalling the objects. Voila, I have confirmed my original hypothesis. Short-term memory is affected by a person's height."

They all looked at me in disbelief. To take this to the next level, I asked if my conclusion made sense.

"Of course not," said Lynn. "It's silly. Everyone knows that memory has nothing to do with a person's height."

"Also," said Diane, "you are only looking at people from this party. And you have to admit they are a pretty weird group."

"OK," I responded. "Let's continue with Lynn's thought. If it doesn't make sense that height affects memory, how else can we explain why my research found that short people have superior short-term memory?"

"I don't know," said Diane.

"My background is in Sociology," I said. "Sociologists are interested in explaining attitudes, belief systems, and behavior based in part on the social structure or social groups to which a person belongs. Therefore, as a Sociologist, I might conclude that short people tend to sit in the front of the classroom, and it is more likely that the teacher will ask them a question. To prepare for this eventuality, they develop short-term memory skills."

"That doesn't make sense either," said Diane.

"OK, if that doesn't make sense, let's try a different approach. What explanation would a psychologist interested in personality development come up with to explain our height and memory findings? Don't be shy. If my sociological explanation is ridiculous, can anybody explain the difference in short-term memory based on different personalities? Give me a tongue-in-cheek explanation of why short people have better short-term memory than tall people."

"Short people have to compensate for their lack of height," said Craig.

"That's a good explanation," I replied. "And it's often referred to as the Napoleon Syndrome. What might somebody interested in the medical sciences, such as a medical doctor, physiologist, or neurologist, conclude?"

Dave said, "It takes the blood longer to reach a tall person's brain."

Diane suggested that women, who tend to be shorter, have superior brains.

"Excellent," I said. "We have come up with several quite different and admittedly silly explanations to explain why short people perform better on a memory test than tall people.

"Now let's look again at the real world and the research on memory and age. I have looked at some of this research, and in general, it supports the assumption that age has a negative effect on short-term memory. Interestingly, age seems to positively affect long-term memory, but that is another issue. The main issue is that when researchers compare two groups of people who differ by age, and when they find differences in memory scores, they assume that age causes these differences. I question this assumption."

To further this thought, I asked, "Can anyone think of another explanation, other than age, that might explain why older people do not do as well on short-term memory tests?"

This caused a moment of silence, and Lynn said, "Is it because our brains have more information; we have more to remember?"

"I'm afraid not," I replied.

To give them a hint, I asked, "When somebody researches memory and age, where do you think the young subjects in this research come from?"

"School, they're students," Lynn replied.

"Of course, and what should university students devote their time to? Studying, naturally, so we find that the young people who take part in this research are university students who spend most of their time exercising their short-term memory. Besides, students are used to writing exams and do not feel intimidated by researchers in lab coats. No wonder they do better on short-term memory tests.

"The older subjects, on the other hand, do not exercise their short-term memory as often or as intensely as the younger students, and many are not as comfortable in a research situation.

"It is quite possible that you start to forget things as you age. However, the reason is not necessarily the aging process or mind deterioration. It is because you do not exercise your short-term memory as much as you used to.

"When you were younger, you learned new things every day. You were learning how to perform your job, meeting new people, remembering which child wants what sandwich in their lunch when to take the children to hockey practice, piano lessons, and so on. As time passes, when the job becomes second nature and the children leave home, your short-term memory can begin to coast.

"As with most bodily functions," I explained, "short-term memory is a function of use. The adage, 'use it or lose it' applies just as readily to short-term memory as to muscle strength. I have met people who returned to school after their children had grown up. When asked if their short-term memory had improved, without exception, they told me that it had improved significantly. It improved because they were beginning to exercise their short-term memory."

USE IT OR LOSE IT

Neurological research supports this conclusion. In a recently published book entitled The Brain That Changes Itself, the author cites various research studies that confirm that the brain can rejuvenate itself through use, including improvements in memory loss.[2] Expecting to forget things as you grow older can become a self-fulfilling prophecy, hastening the mental decline of the use-it-or-lose-it brain.

In another study of nearly 3000 people aged 65 to 94, those people given ten hours of training in memory, problem-solving, and decision-making tasks over several weeks showed marked and lasting increases in cognitive ability. 'Booster' training sessions received a year later resulted in further improvement in mental function, which persisted for over a year.[3]

For additional support, "The mature brain may lose some of the processing speed and accuracy that the younger brain has, but it isn't inferior. The mature brain organizes differently. Especially when it is adequately challenged, it keeps growing and developing new strengths and assets that the average younger brain cannot compete with because of the reservoirs of knowledge that we have what we sometimes call wisdom."[4]

I suggest a research project for anyone interested in this subject. Many older people have gone back to university. The research would involve a group of young students and a group of older students testing their short-term memory. This way, they would be comparing apples to apples, and I am confident that the older students would do as well as the younger students on a short-term memory test. The conclusion would be that it is not age that affects memory but usage.

If you are starting to forget things, you have several options. You can get involved in activities that will exercise your short-term memory, such as going back to school, joining a theatre group where you have to memorize lines, or you can memorize the phone book. These exercises will improve your short-term memory. Alternatively, and this is my preference, you can stop worrying or blaming your age and accept what is happening - you are not exercising your short-term memory as much as you used to.

I am not denying that some older people experience memory loss due to physiological changes or problems. My point is that when short-term memory begins to fail, you should not consider it a sign that you are getting old or senile. People who worry about their memory convince themselves that something is wrong and that it relates to growing old or being re-tired. Re-tirement can affect short-term memory only if your mind stagnates.

The self-fulfilling prophecy does not always work in a negative direction. "The beauty of the self-fulfilling prophecy," I said, "is that it can work for you rather than against you. If you truly believe, and you should, that re-tirement is like winning a lottery and that you will find worthwhile and enjoyable pursuits, you have a far better chance of succeeding. Don't get bogged down with the Ageist Self-fulfilling Prophecy; don't look for signs to confirm that you are getting old. Instead, look for signs to confirm your advantageous situation. You will find them; they are everywhere."

MID-LIFE CRISIS RE-DEFINED

I turned my attention to Lynn and asked, "If you don't mind my asking, how old are you?"

She smiled, hesitated, and said, "No, I don't mind. I'm 62."

"The reason I asked is I get the impression that your concerns are not solely directed toward re-tirement."

"Well, I guess that's true," she said. "The problem is my life feels flat now. I enjoy being a lawyer, and things are going well, but I don't know. Something is missing. That's why when Dave mentioned re-tirement, it piqued my interest. I realize now that just having money is not enough. I have to find alternatives to keep me busy. However, it's true, I probably won't re-tire for a few years yet."

"It sounds to me, Lynn, that you may be experiencing a mid-life crisis."

"You may be right," she replied.

"In that case, I would happily share my views on this issue. They may give you a new way of making sense of this problem. And even though your re-tirement is a few years away, it might just be a cure for this malaise."

"OK," she replied.

There has been much research on the so-called mid-life crisis and volumes of books written on it. Through my workshop experience, I have developed some insights I wanted to share with Lynn and others. Admittedly, my approach and analysis are somewhat simplistic, but they could shed some light on an issue that can be misunderstood.

Therefore, in response to Lynn's concern, I said, "One way to look at the middle-age crisis is to view it as the systematic elimination of unanswered questions and goals. This may sound somewhat formal, but your future was infinite when you were younger. You had everything to look forward to, and your head was full of questions and expectations about your future. I am sure you wondered if, when, and who you would marry, how many children you would have, what they would be like, where you would live, what type of work you would pursue, how rich you would be, and so on. Your head was full of unanswered questions about what might lie ahead in your future. The last thing on your mind was re-tirement."

"Suddenly, you have reached a point where most of your unanswered questions have been answered - some to your satisfaction and others not. You know if and whom you would marry, how rich you would be, and so on. The only main unanswered question that lies ahead is re-tirement, the last thing on your mind when you were younger. If you are unsatisfied with some aspect of your life and feel it is too late to make any changes, if your life no longer includes many unanswered questions or goals, and the thought of re-tiring scares you, do not lose heart. Re-tirement can be your saving grace.

"Let's take a more critical look at middle age. What exactly does the term imply? To my mind, it suggests a mid-point in the progression from birth to death. This image portrays life as linear, indicating that it follows a straight line based on a single dimension - age. In addition, focusing on a mid-point between birth and death implies that the second half will involve losses and will not be as good as the first half. Middle age is halfway to the end. No wonder it can be scary.

"The good news is this description is not accurate. Life experiences from the past and into the future are not linear nor based solely on age. People are not one-dimensional. Our incomes, levels of education, individual skills, confidence levels, family status, and net worth, to name but a few, change over the life span and will continue to change into the future. At certain points, any of these dimensions may be on the rise, on a level plane, or in decline. We are the total of our experiences.

"I do not deny that life can be quite different when you re-tire. However, to reflect the transition process more accurately, I suggest we focus on what I call the 'Centerpoint' of life rather than identifying a mid-point between life and death.

CENTERPOINT

"The Centerpoint is when the individual re-tires with a dash, changes from a work to a re-tirement career and gets a 'new set of wheels'. It involves drawing on past experiences to plan a new career encompassing the best of their work and leisure careers. It doesn't matter how long you process the fusion of your work and leisure careers, the important point is the benefits gained through the process. If you have an exciting re-tirement to look forward to or are experiencing a re-tirement that is worthwhile and enjoyable, you have re-introduced a series of goals and unanswered questions to your life. In so doing, you will either not experience or at least minimize the mid-life crisis."

My reference to Centerpoint is a more accurate way to describe the convergence of your work and leisure careers. This new concept did not exist for past generations because they were less likely to be able to step back and plan for their life following their working career. Today's re-tirees are lucky to have this opportunity. In addition, you do not have to be re-tired to begin this planning process. It should start well before re-tirement.

"I encourage you," I continued, "to look on this period of your life not as middle age but as a staging point and the ideal opportunity to prepare yourself for your re-tirement career. Use this opportunity to re-introduce unanswered questions and goals to your life. Your unanswered questions and goals for the future will probably be quite different from those that you eliminated up to this point. In the future, you may wonder how you can apply some of your knowledge and skills to benefit others, how you can satisfy your needs and skills through different activities, how your re-tirement career will unfold, and so on. If you re-introduce questions and goals to your life, you will replace your malaise with optimism."

I had spoken at length about an important issue. To see if my arguments hit home, I asked Dave, "Well, have I convinced you that re-tirement has nothing to do with growing old?"

"You have," said Dave. "I can see that it doesn't mean I will be old when I re-tire. I didn't stop to think of it that way."

"Hearing what you have to say," said Diane, "especially the part about the self-fulfilling prophecy, makes me feel younger."

"That's great," I replied.

"By the way, does anyone know how and why age, rather than performance, determines when a person can or has to re-tire?"

"I think I read somewhere that it started in Germany," said Lynn.

"That's right. Prince Otto Von Bismarck set up the world's first pension plan in Germany in 1889, and benefits began at age 70. There are several interesting side notes to this piece of history. Firstly, most people at that time did not live beyond age 70. Secondly, it established an arbitrary age as the basis for re-tirement and when a person could draw a pension. This has remained until today. Interestingly, Bismarck lived to be 83 and continued to work well beyond his 70th birthday."

"I may still be at work when I am 70," said Dave.

"There's nothing wrong with that," I replied. "As long as you are enjoying it. My main point is that just because we use age to initiate a pension, do not assume that re-tirement relates to aging or getting old. That may have been the case, but conditions today are completely different from the past."

FROM HIPPIES TO YUPPIES, TO.....?

"If you think about it, you should consider yourselves lucky to be re-tiring now rather than in the past."

"What do you mean?" asked Lynn.

"Look at your situation. Why do you think people who re-tire now or who will soon re-tire are better off compared to retirees in the past?"

"I suppose they'll have more money," Dave answered.

"For sure," I said. "On average, you are richer than any generation of retirees. While you were developing your career, private and public pension plans enabled you to establish an adequate financial base for re-tirement, and you were aware of the need to save and invest for re-tirement.

That's why you found a financial planner."

"Anything else?" I asked.

"We are healthier, and people today will live longer," Craig replied.

"Absolutely, science and medicine have progressed to control or eliminate many diseases, and it has become part of our culture to watch what we eat and to exercise."

I added, "The Boomers are also lucky because they are more educated and have a greater sense of personal fulfillment with greater expectations for fulfillment in re-tirement compared to past generations of retirees. Finally, there are more Boomers than any generation of retirees in the past. This gives them political and economic clout."

"So," I re-emphasized, "you are lucky to be re-tiring now rather than in the past."

"I guess so," said Dave. "But I don't think it was all luck. We worked hard to be able to re-tire."

"I don't mean lucky in that sense," I said. "Don't forget, I defined the new re-tirement as an earned career. And implicit in the word 'earned' is that you did not rely entirely on luck."

I directed my comment to Dave and said, "Do you remember the old image of retirement (without the dash) that we discussed earlier - retirement as withdrawal from work? Well, there was some truth in that image in the past. But because of various conditions that did not exist a generation or two ago, I think you are lucky to re-tire now rather than in the past."

"If you think about it," I said, "we don't have a name or word to describe the Boomers when they re-tire. When the Boomers were younger, they were called Hippies and became Yuppies. So, the question is, what shall we call them when they re-tire?"

COHORT AND A GENERATION

To respond to this question, first, we must define two concepts that often need clarification - a cohort and a generation. A cohort refers to everyone born during a specific period. The Boomers are a cohort that includes everyone born between 1946 and 1964. A generation includes everyone who shares common cultural or social characteristics and attitudes. Hippies are an example of a generation.

The term Hippies referred to a way of thinking and a set of values relating to their lifestyle of political activism, cannabis, peace, the new age, music and art. Of course, not all young people at that time displayed the so-called Hippie lifestyle, but the term applied to the entire Boomer cohort in the past.

When Boomers entered the workforce, their behavior and attitudes changed. Most pursued careers and spent money with a vengeance, and the term "Yuppie" emerged. This stood for Young Urban Professionals and related to their education, work, and living status. Again, not all working Boomers were urban professionals, but the label became commonplace.

"When the Boomers re-tire," I continued, "Yuppies will be obsolete. They are no longer young, many will not live in urban areas, and they will no longer be at work when they re-tire. We need a new term to describe all re-tired Boomers, regardless of their educational, economic, and attitudinal differences."

"We can call them re-tired Boomers," said Diane.

"That's one way to look at it," I replied. "But do you remember why I said you were lucky to be re-tiring now?"

"Sort of," Dave said. "We are richer and will live longer. There were other reasons, but I can't remember all of them."

"Well, I suggest we refer to re-tiring Boomers as 'Luckies'.

"I guess you are right," said Lynn. "When I look at my parents' or grandparents' generation, things are definitely better now."

"Additionally, who knows what the future holds," I added. "Things may not be as good for future generations of re-tirees. So you are lucky to be re-tiring now."

"But another important advantage," I continued, "is that society's image of re-tirement is changing for the better, which will influence your self-image as a re-tiree. Re-tirement is becoming something to be proud of, based mainly on economic considerations."

I explained that each segment of society develops and retains a sense of self-importance, or lack of importance, partly due to its economic buying power. Pre-Boomer retirees were not significant in terms of numbers. They did not live very long after retirement (without the dash), did not have economic clout, and did not represent a market large enough to be pursued by the providers of goods and services. Previously, advertising aimed at older people generally focused on health aids and other non-retirement entities. TV in the past rarely included retired people, and if they did, it was negative. It was as though they did not exist.

"But things will be different when you re-tire," I said. "You represent a huge identifiable market. The suppliers of clothing, entertainment, cosmetics, food, cars, motorcycles, and travel, to name but a few, will continue to court you, especially in re-tirement. When the Boomers were younger, to attract their attention, advertising agencies portrayed happy, lively, healthy, sexy, young people enjoying whatever it was they had to sell. This enabled the Boomers to develop a strong positive image of being the most advantageous group in society. Do you remember the phrase 'never trust anyone over 30'? This arrogance reflected a sense of self-importance spawned by the economic power of the Boomers when they were young. It was easy to feel proud of being a Hippie and a Yuppie because they held economic and political power.

"The beauty of re-tiring now is the Boomers will retain their political and economic clout into re-tirement, and the suppliers of goods and services will continue to court them with vigor. As a result, they will portray retirees differently from the past. They will be seen as happy, lively, healthy, sexy, older people enjoying whatever advertisers wish to sell to this economically powerful cohort."

I told them to think of the significance of this shift and how it will affect society's image of re-tirement. When the Boomers re-tire, they will consist of millions of people with nothing but time and money on their hands, and they are just itching to find happiness that eluded many of them while they were at work. I am willing to bet the barn that the image of re-tirement is in for a dramatic change.

"The signs are everywhere," I said. "Why do you think the major clothing manufacturers introduced loose-fitting or relaxed jeans a few years ago? Do you think this is simply a fashion statement? When I was a kid, loose-fitting jeans were called 'huskies'. If you had to buy huskies, you couldn't fit into regular-fitting jeans. Today, clothing manufacturers want to continue selling to us, but many of us need huskies, and the word huskies is not flattering. The manufacturers repackaged huskies as 'relaxed' fitting to overcome this conundrum. The product is the same; only the name and image have changed."

"I know of another example," said Lynn. "Until a few years ago, my son and I drove to Florida every winter. We stopped at a particular fast-food restaurant as part of our routine. A few years ago, we stopped at a certain restaurant, and they had an area called Play Land. Now they split that for the kids on one side and a player piano on the other."

"That's a good example," I said. "The fast-food industry has realized the importance of older Boomers as customers and has begun accommodating their interests. This is the tip of the iceberg. We see the popularity of music from the 60's and 70's. If you flip through the radio dial, it seems as though there are as many stations playing hits from the past as those playing today's music. Additionally, if you check the newsstand, you will find many new magazines that cater to re-tirees. This was unheard of in the past."

"That makes sense," said Lynn. "But it may be easier said than done."

Dave said to Lynn, "Diane and I went through the Life Goal Planning program with our friends a few weeks ago. It has given me some guidance, and I am beginning to see more clearly what I can do when I re-tire."

"It's never too early to begin thinking about how you will spend your time and how to satisfy your needs and skills in re-tirement," I said.

At that point, Dave's grandson came over and pulled him away from the discussion. As the party began to break up, I excused myself and withdrew to find my wife.

CHAPTER SUMMARY

- Re-tirement is not an aging issue.

- To re-tire is to change from a work to a re-tirement career and if you believe that when you re-tire you are getting old or that others will think of you that way, you are guilty of the Ageist Self-fulfilling Prophecy. That is, you may look for signs to prove or validate your belief and if you look hard enough, you will find them even if you have to create them.

Chapter 8

WITH A LITTLE HELP FROM MY FRIENDS
(The Beatles, 1967)

Spousal Relations and Single in Re-tirement

"You bet. Retirement is great."

The phone rang in my office, and it was Janice. "I don't know if you remember me," she said, "I am Les's wife. We met at Dave and Diane's house about a month ago."

"Of course I remember, Janice. What can I do for you?" I asked.

She confessed that she was having a problem with Les. She sounded worried, so I asked her to explain the problem.

"I didn't want to talk about this when we met at Diane's house," she said, "but there are two problems. Les is always underfoot, and I don't know what to do. Now he is talking about moving, and I'm not sure I want to go."

RETIRED HUBBY A NUISANCE

I found an extreme example in a newspaper advice column many years ago. It was entitled Retired Hubby a Nuisance.

I have been married for 40 years to a man who has changed completely since he retired 10 months ago, and I need to know what to do. He says he is too young for 'senior citizens' and too old to take up a hobby, so he has devoted himself to making my life miserable by hanging over my neck 24 hours a day. I'm ready for the funny farm. The man never boiled water before. Now he thinks he is a great cook. Nothing I prepare tastes right. He has to go grocery shopping with me and decide on everything I put in the cart. He never bought his own underwear, and I had to fight with him to get a new suit and buy shoes. Suddenly he's an authority on everything. When the phone rings, he runs to answer, although no one ever calls him, and he stands around while I talk. When the conversation is over, he wants to know all the details. He never gave a damn before. The last straw was this week when the car insurance came due. He never said a word to me – just sold my car. Please tell me what to do. My daughter is on his side. She says I am lucky to have a husband who is in such good health. Meanwhile, I am – Worn Out and Weary.

Here is the columnist's reply:

Retirement can be depressing and disruptive (especially for wives), but your husband sounds like he might have a neurological problem. Such radical changes in behavior may be organic. Ask your husband's doctor to instruct him to see a neurologist. If he checks out, I hope you will seek counseling for yourself. You can't handle this problem alone; you'll crack up.

I doubt this advice would appear today, but it is an excellent example of a misguided and false image of retirement. It's what I called retirement without the dash and of certain writers, in this case, a journalist, making false assumptions about the relationship between retirement and health. The suggestion that the husband in the article should see a neurologist assumes that retirement is a disease. Re-tirement does not cause brain or nerve damage; it would be a waste of everyone's time for him to see a neurologist. The advice that the wife seeking counseling is also a waste of time because the problem lies with the husband's behavior, and nothing will be gained if the wife sees a counselor.

I asked Janice what she thought was the problem.

"I don't know," she replied. "But it has become my problem, too."

"If you think back to what we talked about at Diane's house," I said, "it seems to me that the problem is obvious. Les is looking desperately for something to do; he's bored."

"I couldn't agree with you more," said Janice. "But what can we do?"

I had a few suggestions to help her situation, but it would be best to include Les in the discussion. I suggested that they both meet at my office the following week. I suggested she tell him we could meet again to see how his re-tirement was progressing. We could talk about this issue and his thoughts about moving. Janice was delighted with my suggestion.

When she and Les came to my office the following week to begin the conversation, I asked Les how re-tirement was progressing. He told me he was applying some of the exercises we went through and was thinking about moving. I took this as my cue and asked where he planned to move.

"Janice and I love the outdoors, so we were thinking about moving west to be near the mountains."

"You mean you were thinking about moving," Janice said to Les. "I'm not so sure. I told Les the other day I was not sure I would be happy to leave here. We have our friends, and our daughter and her family live here."

"But if we move," Les responded, "we can be closer to Richard and his family. There are a few things Janice and I have been trying to come to grips with since I re-tired. Moving is just one of them. The biggest problem is Les is always underfoot. I keep telling him to find something else to do, but it doesn't seem to work."

Les responded, "I admit I have been spending a fair amount of time at home. But some of my best friends are still working."

"This can present problems," I said. "And there is no question that re-tirement can affect the marriage relationship. So, if you would like, I will review some of the points worth considering on this issue."

"I think that would be a good idea," said Janice.

"So do I," said Les. "But is this a common problem?"

"I wouldn't say it's common," I replied. "But re-tirement can change the ground rules in a marriage, and you must spend a little time thinking about the amount and quality of time you spend together."

I explained that when a family is young, most of the leisure time is spent with the children. As time passes, with the children growing up and leaving home and the husband and wife re-tiring, the daily rhythm of time together and apart will likely change. With the freeing up time no longer occupied by work, an adjustment in the time a couple spends together may be necessary.

COMMUNICATION

"One of the most important things you both have to look at," I explained, "is communication, and true communication is crucial when planning for re-tirement."

I had no idea of the inner workings of their marriage, so I spoke about this in general terms and shared an example from a workshop with them. In this case, we discussed housing, and I asked for a show of hands from those considering moving after re-tirement. Several people raised their hands, including one man whose wife turned to him and said with a somewhat surprised look, 'I didn't know we were thinking of moving!'

They both smiled at this point, and I said, "It is fairly safe to assume that they were not communicating about re-tirement."

"But Janice and I have talked about moving," said Les.

"Yes, I realize that," I replied. "I gave this as an example of a couple not communicating their re-tirement plans. My main point is regardless of the level of communication between a couple, re-tirement is a necessary topic of discussion because it is a shared experience, and the more you know of each other's feelings, the more likely the transition is to go smoothly. So, sit down together and clarify your feelings. Talk about how you plan to spend your time. What you plan to do apart and what you plan to do together. You may not have an immediate answer to these questions, but it is important to start thinking and talking in this direction."

I turned to Janice and asked, "When you talked to Les about this problem, were you criticizing him or discussing a solution to the problem?"

"I don't know the solution," she replied. "So, I guess I have been criticizing him. We tried to talk after the session with you but didn't get very far."

"That's OK," I said. "It's a start, and Les may have felt frustrated by his situation, affecting his ability to talk about it. I have a suggestion that may help, but first, let's look at the second issue: Janice's concern that you are interfering with her domain."

"That's a good way to put it," said Janice.

RESPECT EACH OTHERS TERRITORY

I turned to Les and said, "Let me ask you a question. Suppose you were still working. How would you feel if Janice came to work with you and began criticizing and telling you how to improve things?"

Les smiled but did not answer my question. As you can imagine, when I ask this question in my workshop, it hits the nail on the head, and a lively discussion usually follows. To emphasize my point further, I told them the story of Howard. He was happily re-tired, involved in civic duties, and loved to spend time in his basement workshop. One day, when his wife was out, he rearranged the kitchen to make it more efficient.

When his wife came home, she never said a word. Howard assumed that she was pleased with his interior design capabilities. Later, when he was out for the day, his wife went into his workshop and rearranged his tools as she thought they should be arranged.

"With this example," I said, "although Howard's wife did not say anything, she was communicating. Her message was - don't touch my stuff. I met another woman whose husband had taken over the household duties when he re-tired, and she was concerned that he would not return them to her when she re-tired.

"Les, I am not suggesting that you steer clear of Janice's domain. I know some husbands who get involved in the kitchen or housework, and the wife is delighted. My only suggestion is that you discuss this issue with Janice. Please sit down and rationally examine the extent to which Janice would feel comfortable having you get involved in her domain. Let's face it, Les, I imagine that Janice has done a great job up until now. Just because you are re-tired doesn't necessarily mean you can interfere.

"As you both know," I said, "to come up with a solution, you must understand the problem."

"The problem is," said Janice, "Les is interfering with my life."

I turned to Les and asked, "Would you agree that this is an accurate assessment of the problem?"

"I suppose so," he responded.

"Then the solution is for you to find interests that are not simply 'busywork.' As we discussed a few weeks ago, you must find activities that will enable you to replace the satisfaction lost from work and not interfere with Janice's life. Would you say that would be the solution to the problem?" I asked.

"Most definitely," said Janice.

"What do you think, Les?" I asked.

"I guess so," he replied. "For instance, I have enjoyed playing bridge for years. I would love it if Janice joined me. She tried it, but she didn't like it. That might solve part of the problem. But I can't seem to convince her to try."

I replied with a question. "Les, what do you think the chances are of Janice enjoying bridge after you re-tired if she didn't like it before you re-tired? What does your re-tirement have to do with it?"

"I don't know," said Les. "I was just hoping she would like it."

"Am I correct in assuming that you are a pretty good bridge player and Janice would be a beginner?" I asked. "That may be why she didn't like it."

"Well, that's true," replied Les. "But I encouraged her to take lessons, and she didn't want to."

"Well, I think you have your answer. You must face the fact that Janice does not share your love of bridge and that your re-tiring will not change her feelings on this issue."

"I guess you are right. There's nothing I can do," Les lamented.

"There is something you can do," I said. "If you think about it, Les, you just mentioned two needs you would like to satisfy when you re-tire. One is to continue playing bridge, and the other is to have Janice join you. You have spent many years playing bridge without her, which may have to continue. However, your desire to share a re-tirement activity with Janice can flourish. The only thing is you will probably have to satisfy this need through a different activity. Re-tirement gives both of you the freedom to develop a new activity together, which you are both starting anew. This way, you can satisfy your need to do something together, even though it is not through playing bridge.

"If you want to start something new together, you can approach this like I showed you at Dave and Diane's house the other day. In this case, you should look at the other person's Needs and Skills List and develop a combined list that includes needs and skills that apply to both of you. Then brainstorm an activity that you can both take part in."

I explained further, "I don't want you to get the wrong impression. You two indeed have a few things to work out, but eventually, you will find that the freedom of re-tirement will enhance your relationship. Nevertheless, the bottom line, Les, is you have to start applying the tools we went through at Dave's house. You can't rely on Janice to pick up where work left off. It's not fair, and likely, it's not possible."

SINGLE IN RE-TIREMENT

Not everyone is in a couple situation before or after they re-tire. Approximately 44% of seniors are single (widowed, never married, separated or divorced), and this is based on midlife divorce, outliving a spouse, or choosing not to marry. Because women tend to live longer and marry younger than men, they are more likely to be single in re-tirement. On the other hand, many men and women may choose to be single before or after they re-tire. But let's start by looking online.

If you Google this topic, most results focus on the financial side, especially to start planning early and educate yourself. This is good advice. But on the non-financial side, in addition to dating sites for single re-tirees, one finds topics that include Staying healthy, Dealing with divorce, Looking for work, Looking for love, Social & emotional well-being, Housing needs, and Travel.

Yes, these can be important, but most generally apply to life and are not exclusive to re-tirement. Being single by choice or not, whether this situation is desirable or not, extends beyond the scope of re-tirement. Nevertheless, to see how Life Goal Planning can add a fresh approach to this situation, when you complete the Life Goal Planning Workshop (Part 2 of the workbook), check out the Single in Re-tirement exercise at the end of the workshop instructions.

FRIENDSHIPS

I wanted to mention a statement Les made earlier so I said, "Les, if I recall correctly, did you indicate that one of your problems is that some of your friends are still at work?"

"Yes," he replied. "I have to admit it. I miss going to work and seeing my friends."

"That's perfectly understandable," I said. "Let's face it. You have spent a long time at work and probably made quite a few good friends. These are people you saw almost everyday, and you share many common experiences. They can sympathize with you when something goes wrong at work, and can truly appreciate when something goes right. On the other hand, there may be people at work who you are happy never to see again. In any case, your work experience is the basis of a common bond, and when this is missing, as can happen with re-tirement, it can affect friendships."

"The question that many people must face," I explained, "is what might become of their friendship when they re-tire? For example, because you are out of the picture you will not be aware of many changes in the workplace and this may affect the nature of your friendship. You may know of someone who re-tired and continues to show up at work just to keep up with what is happening there."

"I'm one of them," admitted Les. "At least I used to do that but I don't do that any more. But like you said, some of my friends, like Dave, are still at work and I don't get to see them as much as I used to."

"It is also possible," I said, "that if you and a friend from work re-tired at the same time, your re-tirement careers may develop in different directions."

"I suppose that's true," said Les.

RE-TIREMENT MENTORS AND FRIENDSHIPS

Giving up contact with colleagues and patients can be particularly problematic. It was the most frequently mentioned drawback to re-tirement, it was a key reason for working in re-tirement, and the most frequently mentioned loss from work. Here are a few examples.

Main drawback is related to change of geography regarding living. I am too far away from friends to see them on a casual basis. I have to plan a trip of an entire day to see them for social activities. While I am at work or work related activities there are plenty of social resources. It is only after work or on the weekends when it is difficult.

Miss interaction with my patients who were my friends, but they wish me well in this new phase of life. We live in a great little town, have met many wonderful people, and have yet to be bored. We have retained friends from pre-retirement days, and still see them.

Missing seeing our simply wonderful patients, many of whom, became dear friends!

"The main point," I continued, "is that now may be a good time to solidify your present friendships and to expand your friendship circle. For some people, this will not be a problem. However, for others, this is easier said than done. So, why not set out on a campaign? Extend yourself a little. Be willing to take some risks. Seek people out. Talk to them. Start a conversation with someone at a meeting or ball game. This ties in nicely with Les's search to find re-tirement activities. Join a club, take a course at a community college, volunteer for something, or join a health club. Do whatever it takes to get in touch with new people, your source for companionship, support, approval, security, encouragement, and affection. You never know what will come out of this until you try."

CHAPTER SUMMARY

- Key issues to look at include communication, respecting each other's territory, and creating activities together.

- Communication is critical in the decision for both spouses to re-tire at the same time.

- Giving up contact with colleagues can be particularly problematic. It was the most frequently mentioned drawback to re tirement, a key reason for working in re-tirement, and the most frequently mentioned loss from work.

Chapter 9

OUR HOUSE
(Graham Nash, 1970)

Moving in Re-tirement

Janice's concern about moving is a common issue in re-tirement. The problem is that the more traditional approach seems to miss the most important elements of this issue. For instance, it is common to focus on the pros and cons of various types of housing (e.g. condominiums, apartments, co-ops, mobile homes, re-tirement communities, and so on). I call this the real estate approach. This issue may be important, but it ignores the more critical issues, like the one faced by Janice and Les, in the context of changing from a work to a re-tirement career. Their concern goes beyond the real estate issue.

BEWARE OF GENERALITIES

Within the traditional approach, housing issues are often subject to generalities. For example, a couple who participated in my workshop told me about a course they attended. The speaker referred to a stress level chart stating that retirement was a high-stress situation. As such, the speaker warned that one should not consider moving until at least one year following retirement.

To re-quote an expression I used earlier – hogwash. This is a classic 'retire without the dash' blanket statement. There are three things wrong with this statement. First, it is a sweeping generalization, which has no place in re-tirement planning. Second, re-tirement is not necessarily a high-stress situation. In many cases, re-tirement can lower stress. Third, moving at re-tirement is often a wise decision.

Not everyone wants to move at retirement. Many prefer to stay where they are and do not want to move. However, retirement can also be a time of positive change. In fact, it can be the perfect time to change your housing situation. Many people at our workshop actively consider moving after they retire. Some think about moving to a small town or a cottage; others think about returning to their birthplace. Many plan to spend the winter in a warmer climate, while others plan to move to a different – usually smaller – home or condominium within the same city or community. I even met a couple at a workshop who built a bigger house in retirement. Everyone has different needs and priorities, and it is clear that the decision to move goes well beyond financial or real estate considerations. Moving after retirement requires careful consideration, especially if, as in Janice's case, one person wants to move and the other does not.

Rather than tell Les and Janice what they should do, I wanted to inform them of a few housing considerations contributing to re-tirement happiness. I turned to Les and said, "You mentioned that you would like to move, but it seems this may present problems for Janice. Why do you want to move?"

"I think we would be better off if we move," said Les.

"Better off in what way?" I asked.

"We can save money by moving to a smaller community, and we love the outdoors. We usually spend our summers camping and fishing and love skiing. I don't have a spot picked out yet. Nevertheless, if we moved to a small city near the mountains, we would have the best of both worlds.

Besides, if we sold our house, we would have more money to live off."

"Your reasoning sounds good," I said. "But the problem is, it doesn't seem to be in sync with Janice's plans. So, let's look at Janice's concern and see if you can find a solution or at least a compromise."

I asked them if they knew anyone who moved after re-tirement and who, after moving, realized it was a mistake.

"Well, yes," said Les. "This guy I worked with and his wife moved back to England. They stayed about six months and didn't like it. I heard that they moved back."

"Like all issues in re-tirement," I said, "just because you know of one case where a plan did not work out, it does not necessarily follow that it will not work out for you. We can learn a few things from your friend's experience, and the decision to move should not be treated lightly."

I advised them to consider two very important questions. First, can you satisfy your needs and skills in the new community? Second, if it doesn't work out, what are your alternatives? You don't want to feel trapped there.

"Sometimes it's impossible to predict what it will be like living in a new community," I said, "until after the move. You have to expect the unexpected. You may miss old friends, the doctor, and dentist who looked after you for years, your mechanic you trust, your standing in the community, and familiar places filled with memories. And then again, re-tirement is a great opportunity for a new beginning."

My main concern was that they thought this through thoroughly and reached a mutually agreed-upon compromise. To start their thinking, I told them about Sylvia, who moved and encountered an unexpected problem. Here's what happened.

Sylvia was a widow. After she re-tired, she moved back to a small town where she came from to be near her family. She always enjoyed holidays back home, so moving home seemed like a good idea now that she could live where she wanted. At first, things went well, but after a while, she felt stifled by her family. They always thought about her and were concerned that she was not lonely. Therefore, whenever her family members entertained, they always included Sylvia. When she entertained, she felt obliged to invite her family.

However, Sylvia wasn't lonely. She wanted to develop new friendships outside her family sphere, but constantly being with her family kept her from developing new friendships. She wasn't meeting anyone new because she lived in a small town. Her friendships were limited. She longed for the sense of independence she used to feel. Unfortunately, she had sold her original home, housing prices began to rise, and she couldn't afford to buy another house in her former community. She eventually moved back to the city she used to live in, rented an apartment, and continues to visit her family for special occasions only - as she used to do before she re-tired.

After I finished relating this story to Les and Janice, they looked a little pensive.

"I'm not trying to talk you out of moving," I said. "I'm just warning you to be cautious when moving because you never know what it will be like until you move there."

RE-TIREMENT MENTORS

Twenty-two percent of your re-tirement mentors moved after they re-tired. Of these, 72% moved far enough away that they had to establish new friends. Re-tirement can be the perfect time to change your housing situation, however it should involve careful consideration. Having said that, the housing market can add a new wrinkle to the decision to re-tire as some people may be relying on selling their home to help finance their re-tirement. Chart 9-1 includes the main reasons your re-tirement mentors decided to move.

One thing that stands out is there are many reasons beyond the standard reasons for moving presented on Chart 9-1. Here are a few examples of 'Other' reasons for moving.

Build house of dreams where I always wanted to live.

Closer to our cottage.

Could no longer afford two mortgages.

Chart 9-1. Reasons for Moving

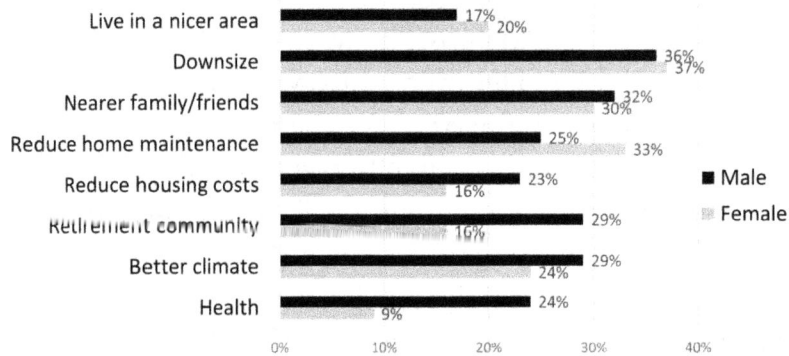

Reason	Male	Female
Live in a nicer area	17%	20%
Downsize	36%	37%
Nearer family/friends	32%	30%
Reduce home maintenance	25%	33%
Reduce housing costs	23%	16%
Retirement community	29%	16%
Better climate	29%	24%
Health	24%	9%

■ Male
▨ Female

Different life style.

For change of lifestyle -- we currently live on an island in (the Caribbean).

Get away from crowding in a big city..

I moved back home.

I needed the physical change to allow myself the new freedom.

Lots of outdoor activities where we moved.

Moved to own home from temporary accommodation provided by employer.

My practice was attached to the house.

Retired to cottage, long term plan.

Snow skiing and living in the mountains.

To a college town, more activities than small town I practiced in.

To an assigned location, then returned to same house of 30 years.

To live on a lake, own a boat, be near kids and grand kids.

To return to area where grew up - a smaller community and less hectic pace.

Tore down family cottage and built new.

DON'T BE IMPULSIVE

To give them some guidelines, I said, "We can learn a few things from Sylvia's story. If you decide to move, the best advice I can give you is to be careful, not too impulsive, and not burn your bridges. Don't buy a home before knowing that it is right for you. This can lead to grief."

I told them about Greg and Sara's experience. They lived in the Midwest and took a holiday to visit their children who lived on the coast. After spending a week with the kids, they took a side trip to a small town a few hours away. They came across a small house overlooking the ocean, and Greg loved it. According to Sara, Greg was all set to buy. This would be the re-tirement home of his dreams. She wasn't sure, so she suggested they wait until they could survey the area properly. They went back to spend a few more days with their children. Then they returned to that small town and, after spending a few days there, realized this location was not right for them. It would have been a big mistake if they had impulsively bought it impulsively. Fortunately, Sara had the foresight to hold back on Greg's impulse.

"Buying impulsively can be disastrous," I said. "You never know what it will be like - or what you might miss - until you spend some time there."

I told them about a couple I met who moved from a big city to a small community. After a while, they began to miss their former neighbors. Although they used to live in a large city, they were part of a very tight community where they had very close ties. When they realized their mistake, they went back to their original neighborhood, hoping to find a house to buy. They went door-to-door, asking if anyone wanted to sell. Unfortunately, no one was willing. Eventually, they bought a house four blocks away, but it was not the same. Being somewhat removed, they could not regain the tight friendships they gave up.

SATISFY YOUR NEEDS IN THE NEW COMMUNITY

"Another important rule," I stressed, "is to ask yourself if you can satisfy your needs and skills in the new community. Can you find activities that are worthwhile and enjoyable? Of course, you may never know until you move. But this important condition should be kept in mind."

"As I mentioned, we like to do things outdoors, so I don't think this will be a problem for us," said Les.

"You never know," I replied. "Let me tell you about somebody who encountered this problem after moving. His name is Stan, and before he re-tired, he and his wife used to spend the winters in a resort town in California. They thought that this would be the perfect place to re-tire. The weather was good, they both enjoyed playing golf, and they developed a small group of friends over the years. So, when Stan re-tired they sold their house and purchased a small house in this community. They spent some time fixing it up, and about a year later, they sold the house and bought a condominium. Six months later, they sold the condominium and bought another house.

"It became clear that their series of moves was not strictly a housing issue. Stan was bored and kept busy by moving and fixing up the houses he bought. Sure, he enjoyed golfing and various other activities, but they didn't totally replace being at work. To compensate for this, he worked at moving. He didn't do this to make money; he was looking for something to keep him busy. Eventually, they moved back to their original home city, Stan became involved in a small business, and they have not moved since. They still visit California and thoroughly enjoy life."

DON'T BURN YOUR BRIDGES

"Do you own your home?" I asked.

"Yes, we do," said Janice.

"Then the next advice I can offer is if you move, 'don't burn your bridges.' Don't sell everything without giving your newly adopted home a trial run. If possible, rent out your present home and rent a place in the region where you plan to move. This may not be comparable to owning a home in the new community but think of it as insurance. After your trial period, you will then be able to judge what is best for you. If it doesn't work out, you still have your original house to move back to. If it works out, make the move permanent by selling your house. Who knows, your house may be worth more after renting it out for six months or a year. And by renting initially in the new community, you have flexibility after you learn more about where you want to live."

"Another piece of advice," I continued, "which may not apply to you, is don't succumb to pressures from well-meaning friends or even your children. You be the judge. Think about the lifestyle you want and the kind of people you are."

I told them about a couple I met who lived in a large house that was becoming a burden to both. They were spending too much time cleaning and repairing things around the house. They had dreams of moving to a small farm. Unfortunately, their son did not want them to sell the house. He still lived at home, and if his parents sold the house, he would have nowhere to live. To avoid having to find and pay for his own place, he made his parents feel guilty for wanting to sell the family house.

"That doesn't apply to us," said Les.

"I realize that," I replied. I am telling you about a few situations I have encountered because, as I mentioned before, you will never know what problems might come up after you move."

IF THE DECISION IS NOT MUTUAL

"OK," I said. "Let's look at the other slightly thornier issue where Les wants to move, but Janice doesn't."

I told them about Ann who said that her husband was an avid fisherman and hunter. When he re-tired, he wanted to move to a 40-acre property that was at least a 30-minute drive to civilization. Ann told us that she went with her husband to look at the property and she just sat in the car crying. She knew that if they moved there, she would be bored out of her mind and hate every minute of it. She had a dilemma.

It's also possible that one person might want to move back to where they came from, and the other wants to stay where they are. For example, I met a woman in my workshop who mentioned that her husband wanted to return to Bermuda, his birthplace. However, she didn't want to move because she couldn't stand her in-laws. Sometimes those people who think about moving back home forget why they left in the first place. Situations where one person wants to move and the other doesn't may not have an easy solution. To minimize the potential problem, I emphasized to Les and Janice the need for compromise.

"Janice, if you decide to try a move and haven't burned your bridges, do it with an open mind. If you expect to hate the new location, chances are it will become a self-fulfilling prophecy. It will come true. This means that both of you should work towards finding worthwhile and enjoyable pursuits in the new community. If you can satisfy your needs and skills in the new community, the move will probably be a positive experience. If not, and if you are not trapped, you can always move back to where you came from or another location."

People who think about moving after re-tirement may never get this thought out of their system until they try it. So go for it. Having said that, you must be prepared to expect the unexpected and not put yourself in a position where you cannot either come back to where you came from or move on to somewhere else. If it doesn't work out and you can rectify the situation, you will gain from the experience. You will have learned that your original thought of moving was not for you.

"Well," I asked, "has that helped your situation?"

"Yes, it has," said Les. "I still want to move, and I know it might be a problem for Janice. Nevertheless, I think you will agree with me on this, Janice. We both have some things to consider. The most important thing I have learned is that we shouldn't sell our house until we are sure about this move."

"And what are your thoughts on this, Janice?" I asked.

"I was thinking the same thing as Les. I guess I would be more willing to try it, knowing we had something to come back to."

I encouraged Les and Janice to continue discussing what we had talked about. Again, I assured them that many couples have faced similar problems and that they are not insurmountable. They thanked me and left feeling, I believe, optimistic about the future.

ADVICE

Research Before You Move. Explore many sites, especially if you hadn't traveled much during your work years.

Know where you are going and what you are doing.

Know your objectives prior to the move.

Prepare prior to retiring. Check all different areas you are considering prior to retiring.

Research carefully and realize that what you enjoy on vacation, may not fit you full time.

Spend a lot of time looking at every community because they all have pluses but other factors you may find not to your liking. We made a list of things we wanted: 2 car garage, master on first floor, walk out basement, new construction, hardwood floors, etc. and found a development that had everything.

Test the waters before making a commitment to move away from social connections.

Test the waters first by 'renting' (at least 6 months) in your desired area before committing to buying property.

Be sure you are going to be in a location where there is public transportation to a major city. Also, nice to be 10 minutes from a regional medical center. Being in an elevator building is critical for future thinking.

Best to downsize.

Both you and spouse need to agree completely.

Don't go too far away from children.

Forget about your dream home - buy something affordable - with a master bedroom suite on the first floor and something your spouse will be able to maintain when you become disabled or die.

Move to an area with active adult activities.

Move to where you vacation and be on vacation all the time.

Obtain the downsized property while still working. Move in gradually. 'Test drive' the new environs.

Pick a warm climate without much or no snow. It's easier to shovel rain!

Relax for a few months. Think about what you want to do.

Rent, don't buy right away.

Think through what you will do with your days, try out some new activities.

Try the new location for a few seasons.

Be outgoing to obtain new friends.

Get involved with church, service organization, etc. to meet new friends.

Get involved with volunteering, both in general and with dentistry!

If you are deeply involved in other people's lives you will find it a plus, otherwise likely a challenge.

Make sure that you are going to be busy enough to feel fulfilled in life. Although I am quite extroverted is has been difficult to establish a group of individuals for social activities which are non-work related.

Move while you are young enough and are healthy enough to go through the process of making new friends.

Realize that it will take a good long while to re-establish friendships so expect to be lonely for awhile.

CONTINUE THE PROCESS

As I said in the introduction, this book has no definite ending. It ends when you find activities in re-tirement that you consider worthwhile and enjoyable, and this will happen at different times for different people. If you completed the workshop and are using this workbook to supplement the workshop, you are just at the beginning. I encourage you to redo the workshop with your friends, family, work associates, or on your own and to continue to add items to your needs and skills list, and if necessary, brainstorm some re-tirement ideas. If you have not completed the workshop, your next step is to go through the Life Goal Planning process so you can learn how it works. The following section includes complete step-by-step instructions and the necessary worksheets. You could complete this on your own, but I encourage you to get together with a small group, especially for the brainstorming session, as it can be much more effective in a group situation.

Here's to a worthwhile and enjoyable re-tirement!

CHAPTER SUMMARY

- Do not be impulsive in making a decision to move.

- Make sure you consider the opportunity to satisfy your needs in the new location or community.

- Don't burn your bridges. Have a back-up plan if your move doesn't work out.

APPENDIX

In addition to physicians, we surveyed retired dentists, teachers, and police officers. As a matter of interest we can compare professions based on several key factors.

Table 1indicates that:

Physicians: Least likely to work in retirement.

Dentists: Least likely to plan, volunteer, and be very satisfied.

Teachers: Most likely to plan, be very satisfied, and volunteer.

Police Officers: Most likely to work, and move in retirement.

Table 1-1. Profession (%)

	Planning	Very Satisfied	Working	Volunteer	Move
POLICE	59	61	83	65	43
TEACHERS	72	69	57	78	25
DENTISTS	33	52	42	46	20
PHYSICIANS	35	59	34	52	21

Table 2 compares the same factors by location.

Table 1-2. Location (%)

	Planning	Very Satisfied	Working	Volunteer	Move
UNITED STATES	39	58	57	61	25
CANADA	30	60	28	45	19

Life Goal Planning Workshop

A Splendid Time is Guaranteed For All
(The Beatles, 1967)

WORKSHOP INSTRUCTIONS

We have reached a point of transition from theory to practice, so I will use this juncture to describe briefly where we are heading. In pointing out the main drawbacks of re-tirement such as social losses, feeling of boredom, reduced motivation, and so on, keep two things in mind. First, most of the re-tirees in our sample felt that life in re-tirement was as good as or better than life before re-tirement, and most were very or reasonably satisfied with re-tirement. Second, if you are concerned about any of these drawbacks, the Life Goal Planning Workshop includes the tools to help you turn things around.

Understanding the theory behind a worthwhile and enjoyable re-tirement is only the first step. To benefit from your newfound knowledge, you have to apply it in the real world. You had a very brief look at the Life Goal Planning Workshop in Chapter 3, and now I encourage you to complete it yourself on your own or preferably with a group of friends and relatives. You can go through the exercises before or after you re-tire, and once you complete the workshop, keep working at it.

START BY LOOKING FOR CLUES

Adding items to your Life Goal List is like gathering clues to solve a mystery. Initially you gather everything that might be remotely related without judging or evaluating, and then when you sort through your clues you might see a pattern that solves the mystery. Finding worthwhile and enjoyable replacements for work may not exactly be a mystery, but I am sure you get the point. Get together with friends and family to run your own brainstorming session. On the other hand, you could brainstorm some ideas to yourself when you are alone stuck in traffic. Keep your eyes and ears open to new ideas. Watch for how you can add your personal touch to change a humdrum idea into one that is just right for you.

Creating your personal re-tirement Life Goal Plan involves written exercises and a brainstorming session, and you can complete it on your own, or preferably with a small group of friends and relatives. The process of finding worthwhile and enjoyable re-tirement pursuits applies before and after re-tirement, and although the instructional text focuses on the former, if you are re-tired you can interpret it to your situation.

The worksheets are included at the end of the book and numbered from W-1 to W-17. If you are working with a small group, you have permission to photocopy the worksheets for each participant providing you do not use it for commercial use such as in a workshop hosted by an employer, union, or financial organization. Your re-tirement strategy includes the following steps:

1. Calculate Your Re-tirement Lifestyle Readiness Score
2. List Your Re-tirement Plans
3. Identify Your Life Goal
4. Evaluate Your Re-tirement Plans
5. Brainstorm New Plans
6. After the Brainstorming
7. Guide Your Re-tirement Career

STEP 1: CALCULATE YOUR RE-TIREMENT LIFESTYLE READINESS SCORE

If you haven't already done so, start by completing the Re-tirement Lifestyle Readiness Quiz on pages W-2 to W-4. This will establish your starting point. Later when you complete the program you can re-do the quiz to see how much your lifestyle readiness has increased.

STEP 2: LIST YOUR RE-TIREMENT PLANS

Next, write your re-tirement plans on page W-5. How do you plan to spend your time in re-tirement? What activities do you plan to pursue? If you are re-tired, list the activities you pursue. It doesn't matter if your plans are concrete or vague, include them anyway, and write them in your worksheets on the top of page W-5.

STEP 3: IDENTIFY YOUR LIFE GOAL

Your personal Life Goal is your re-tirement wish list that includes your needs, skills, and interests that you wish to satisfy when you re-tire and is the foundation upon which you will create your re-tirement. It establishes the conditions to ensure that your re-tirement will be worthwhile and enjoyable, and it will be the basis for evaluating and creating new plans.

You can identify your Life Goal by answering the following six simple questions about your work and leisure. Write your answers starting on page W-6 in the column headed "Life Goal" as in the following example. Once you complete your Life Goal List, it should look something like the condensed example in Figure 10-1.

Question 1. Needs Satisfied by Work: In Chapter 2, Dave and Diane listed the things they might miss from work when they re-tire, and I asked you to do the same. If you completed this, write your replies on your Life Goal List on page W-6. For example, you might miss friendships, routine, challenge, money, stimulation and so on. If you are re-tired, list the things you miss. The things you might miss are in fact your needs satisfied by work and given that the key to re-tirement happiness is to satisfy these needs, it is very important that you identify these needs.

Question 2. Work Skills: After listing your needs satisfied by work, on the next available lines on page W-6, list the skills you have developed through work. These can be job specific such as writing, public speaking, computer skills, etc., and you are encouraged to include general skills, such

Figure 10-1

W-6	LIFE GOAL	PLAN A	PLAN B
	Social interaction		
	Stimulation		
	Responsibility		
	Computer skills		
	Writing		
	Handyman		
	Creative		
	Holiday		
	Relaxation		
	Home repairs		
	Cooking		
	Bicycle		
	Exploring		
	No hassles		
	Take up golf		

as being good with people, time management, leadership, organizational skills, and so on. These are important because part of the reason we enjoy an activity is because it gives us the opportunity to use and develop our skills, and skills are transferable. Therefore, by identifying your skills at work, you may be able to transfer these to a re-tirement activity.

Question 3. Needs Satisfied by Leisure: Having looked at work, now look at leisure. On the next available line list a current leisure activity, and below it list several reasons (one reason per line) why you enjoy it. Your reasons for enjoying leisure are in fact your needs satisfied by leisure, and together with your needs satisfied by work, they can provide important clues to your re-tirement happiness.

Question 4. Needs Satisfied by Leisure in the Past: This question is similar to question 3, but think about your leisure in the past. Include a leisure activity from the past when you were a kid or before you started working full-time, and then list your reasons for enjoying that activity. Even though you may no longer participate in some past leisure activities, listing the reasons you enjoyed them can identify additional needs.

Question 5. Leisure Skills: Think about the skills you have that you use in the context of your leisure. For example, you might include specific skills such as carpentry, painting, gardening, cooking, or more general skills such as a good listener, or a good letter writer. List any leisure skills that are not already on your list from question 2. Include what others have said you are good at even if these skills seem trivial to you. Put modesty aside and include everything you can think of.

Question 6. Re-tirement Needs: List the things you look forward to when you re-tire but are not already on your list. Your additions may include things like freedom, sleeping-in, travel, more time with your spouse/friends, no hassles, and so on. If you are re-tired, list anything else you enjoy about re-tirement.

Now answer this question. If all the items in your Life Goal List were met in re-tirement, would your re-tirement be worthwhile and enjoyable? I suspect your answer is yes because your list includes your needs, skills, and interests and if these were satisfied in re-tirement, of course it would be worthwhile and enjoyable. Your Life Goal List is very important. It is your re-tirement objective and it identifies the conditions that are necessary for your re-tirement to be worthwhile and enjoyable. It is a measuring rod should you need to make changes or improve things, and it will prove valuable should you want to come up with new ideas or plans for re-tirement. You can also use it as a benchmark to see how your plans match up, because if they don't, later you will learn how to improve them. Now you can put your Life Goal List to work by testing your re-tirement plans.

STEP 4: EVALUATE YOUR RE-TIREMENT PLANS

Your Life Goal List outlines the conditions for a worthwhile and enjoyable re-tirement; therefore, you can use it to test your re-tirement plans. Start by thinking about the plans you wrote on page W-5, refer to your Life Goal List, and ask yourself if each item on your list will meet your re-tirement plans to your satisfaction. Write your responses in the column under Plan A. You can answer 'Y' (Yes), for those items that you expect will be met, 'N' (No), for those you do not expect will be met, or '?' (Question

Figure 10-2

W-6 LIFE GOAL	PLAN A	PLAN B
Social interaction	Y	
Efficient	Y	
Stimulation	?	
Responsibility	Y	
Computer skills	N	
Writing	N	
Handyman	Y	
Creative	Y	
Holiday	Y	
Relaxation	Y	
Home repairs	Y	
Cooking	Y	
Bicycle	N	
Exploring	Y	
No hassles	?	
Take up golf	Y	

mark) for those you are not sure about and have to wait until you re-tire. Think about all your re-tirement plans together, not just a single activity.

For example, suppose my re-tirement plans included spending the winters in a warmer climate, my wife and I were planning to take up tennis, and I thought about finding a part-time job. I look at the first item on my list, and think my need for friendships will be met so I mark it with a Y. But I am not sure that my need for stimulation will be met so I will mark it with a question mark, and so on. Evaluate all items on your list even those that may not be relevant. This is an important part of Life Goal Planning so be honest with yourself; if you do not think an item will be met, identify it appropriately as in the example in Figure 10-2.

LIFE GOAL SHORTFALL

Having tested your re-tirement plans, if you identified any items that will not be met in re-tirement, you have a shortfall in meeting your Life Goal. List on page W-12, the items that are important to you and that you would like to maintain in re-tirement but that you designated with "N" or "?"

To return to my plans, one thing I have learned is my main reason for thinking about a part-time job is to satisfy my need for stimulation and challenge, more so than the money. So I don't want just any job, I want one that will satisfy these needs. What have you learned about your plans?

COMPARE DIFFERENT PLANS

If you are considering two different re-tirement plans, for example finding another job or sticking with your original re-tirement plan, you can evaluate and compare different scenarios. You can use the Plan B column to evaluate finding a job, and compare it with your original Plan A (see Figure 10-3). This example assumes that you have a specific job in mind and are able to determine if it will satisfy your needs and skills. If you do not have a particular job in mind, you may have to include several question marks when evaluating certain Life Goal items such as stimulation, challenge, and so on. Comparing the results may make it obvious which plan is likely to satisfy more of your needs and skills, and hence be more worthwhile and enjoyable.

If you completed the exercises, you have identified your re-tirement objective or your Life Goal, so you know the conditions that will make your re-tirement worthwhile and enjoyable. You have used this valuable information to test your re-tirement plans so you know the quality of your

Figure 10-3

W-6 LIFE GOAL	PLAN A	PLAN B
Social interaction	Y	Y
Efficient	Y	N
Stimulation	?	Y
Responsibility	Y	Y
Computer skills	N	N
Writing	N	N
Handyman	Y	Y
Creative	Y	Y
Holiday	Y	Y
Relaxation	Y	N
Home repairs	Y	Y
Cooking	Y	Y
Bicycle	N	N
Exploring	Y	N
No hassles	?	N
Take up golf	Y	N

plans, whether they will enable you to reach your Life Goal, and if not, the areas that could be improved. You have also learned how to compare re-tirement plans. You are well ahead of others who do not know where they are heading.

STEP 5: BRAINSTORM NEW PLANS

Even if your plans look like they will enable you to reach your Life Goal, conditions could change, they may lose their appeal after the initial euphoria of the 'honeymoon stage' wears off, or you may not have a solid re-tirement plan to begin with. If you are re-tired and feel something is missing, you may be looking for new interests. Whatever your situation now or in the future, the perfect re-tirement activities will not fall into your lap and you have to start somewhere. The best way to start this process is through a brainstorming session and the purpose is to come up with as many initial suggestions or ideas as possible as a starting point for your re-tirement career. You can complete the brainstorming on your own, but it can be much more effective if it is completed with a group as group members make re-tirement suggestions to each other. Get your spouse, friends, and relatives together for the session. The others do not have to complete a Life Goal List to help you out, but if they complete their own lists, you can all take turns brainstorming with each other.

Here's how it works. If we have a group of eight people and if Mary starts, she reads her Life Goal List out loud (Figure 10-4). Meanwhile, the others are each taking notes and writing down what they consider Peter's important needs, skills, and interests. When Mary has finished reading her Life Goal List aloud, each person looks at their brainstorming notes and ties together two or three of her needs, skills, and interests in order to suggest an activity for Mary in re-tirement. For example, if she mentioned travel, gardening, good organizer, and "I like the people I work with," Peter might suggest that she organizes a group to tour gardens in England; Paul might suggest that she gets a job at a garden shop, Sally might suggest she helps the elderly learn to use a computer, and so on.

Figure 10-4

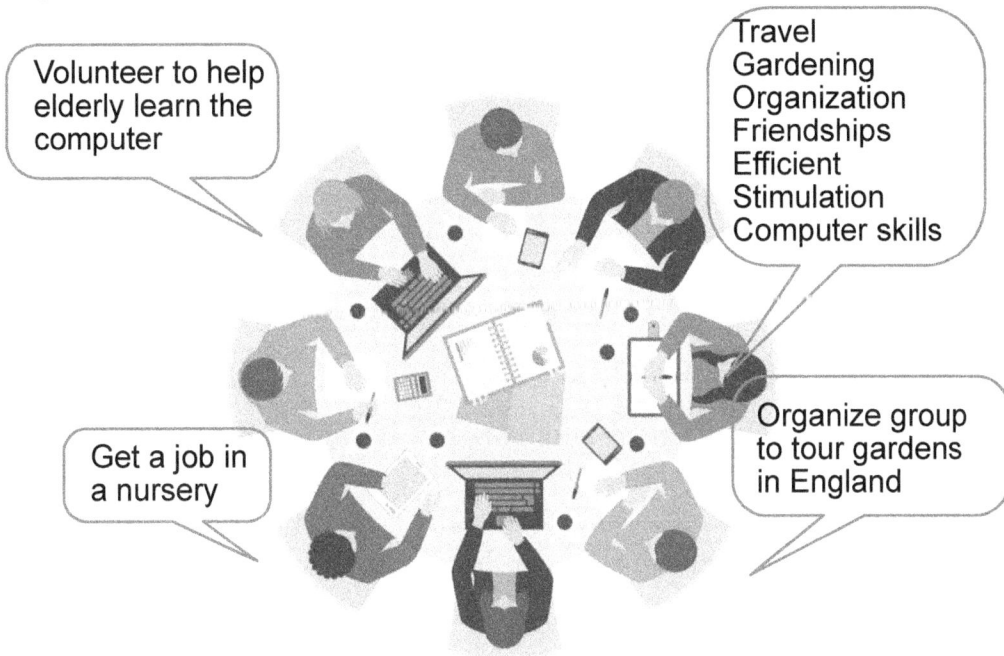

SUGGESTIONS RECEIVED

When suggestions are made, the reader writes the suggestions received on his or her worksheet on page W-10. Do not judge or eliminate a suggestion because it does not appeal to you or you do not think you can do it - just write it down as given. Later you will be instructed on how to interpret the results. For now, just write it down.

SUGGESTIONS GIVEN

When each person makes a suggestion, he or she must write the suggestion he or she gave to the reader on their own worksheets on page W-11. Later you will learn the benefits of writing down your suggestion. Each person is responsible to make at least one suggestion for the person seeking re-tirement ideas. The suggestions do not have to be perfect. This is just a starting point. When making a suggestion, do not ask questions, elaborate on or justify your suggestion. Keep the discussion to a minimum but suggest what you think might satisfy the reader's needs and skills when he or she re-tires. Try to come up with realistic suggestions, and remember - anything goes, be creative, use lateral thinking. With a group of eight people, each person should end up with at least 14 suggestions; 7 suggestions received, and 7 suggestions given.

GROUP FACILITATOR

Each person is to take a turn, and work in a 10-minute time limit, to read, receive, and write his or her suggestions. Pick a timekeeper to ensure that the time limit is adhered to and that both the person who receives and makes a suggestion writes it on their Suggestions Given and Suggestions Received sheet.

BRAINSTORM ON YOUR OWN

To complete this stage on your own you will be wearing two hats – you will be brainstorming re-tirement career suggestions to yourself. The key here is to pretend that the Life Goal List you developed earlier belongs to someone else. Read it and removing yourself, be objective, identify or single out key or important needs and skills. Then brainstorm a few suggestions for re-tirement that you think will satisfy those needs and skills. Try to be totally objective and let the ideas flow. Put aside for the moment your likes, dislikes, abilities, and limitations. Remember, you are brainstorming for a different person. When brainstorming ideas, anything goes. Be creative, use lateral thinking, and suggest what you think might satisfy some of the needs and skills on the list. Every suggestion has the potential of providing you with a clue to enhance your enjoyment in re-tirement. When you make a suggestion, write it on page W-11.

STEP 6: AFTER THE BRAINSTORMING

The main purpose of the brainstorming is to serve as a starting point for improving or creating new plans. Nevertheless, as a valuable secondary benefit it can provide insights to add items to your Life Goal List. We will look first at expanding your Life Goal List.

Now I will let you in on a little secret. Look at page W-11, the suggestions you made to others. You may not realize this, but these suggestions can include very important clues for your benefit and this is why earlier I stressed the importance of writing down both the Suggestions Given and Received. What do you see? Likely, you see some suggestions that appeal to you. The reason for this is when you are making a suggestion to someone else, you are imposing your own interests and needs on that person, and in essence, you are saying, "If I were you, this is what I would do." In fact, you are not that other person, but you may be able to find some important clues among the suggestions you made to that other person. Do you see any suggestions or parts of suggestions that appeal to you? Do you see any patterns in the suggestions you made for others? Did you make several suggestions that involved for example, starting a business, teaching, helping others, or joining something?

If you identify any items, suggestions, or patterns that appeal to you from the suggestions you made to others, add them to your Life Goal List, if they are not already there. Then ask yourself if these additional items will help meet your re-tirement plans. If not, and if they are important to you, include them with your Life Goal Shortfall List on page W-12, and think about how you can improve your plans so that some of these newly identified needs or skills will be met.

For example, I met a welder in a workshop whose re-tirement plans included moving to a farm and opening a welding shop to keep his skills up and earn extra money. During the brainstorming, he made several suggestions to others that involved teaching in areas that focused on the individuals' interests. When he realized this hidden insight, he thought about changing his plans to see if he could somehow teach welding either through the local school or if not, maybe he could teach somebody informally in his workshop. The point is, the idea of teaching had not occurred to him until he made suggestions to others. Can you find any hidden clues in your suggestions to others?

Also, take a close look at your Suggestions Received on page W-10 to see if you can identify any items, suggestions, or patterns that appeal to you. If so, add them to your Life Goal List, and think about how you can improve your plans to meet some of these newly identified needs or skills.

VISUALIZATION EXERCISE

Another exercise that might help to expand your Life Goal List is to select an activity from all the suggestions that appeal to you from the suggestions received and given, and even if it is unrealistic, imagine you are involved in that activity. Ask yourself what you would enjoy about that activity or what needs and skills that activity would satisfy. If you identify any that are not already on your list, add them to your list. Although the activity you are visualizing may be unrealistic, it may reveal additional needs or skills that may be satisfied through a more realistic activity. For example, I recall one workshop participant who visualized being a conductor in a symphony orchestra. When she thought about why she would enjoy this activity, she listed things like being the boss, travel, loving music, and so on. She was then able to add a few of these items to her Life Goal List, which actually gave her a different perspective on her re-tirement. If you added any items to your Life Goal List, ask yourself if these additional items will meet your re-tirement plans. If not, and if they are important to you, add them to your Life Goal Shortfall List (W-12), and ask yourself how you can improve your plans so that some of these new needs or skills will be met.

STEP 7: GUIDE YOUR RE-TIREMENT CAREER

The main purpose of the brainstorming is to come up with as many initial suggestions or ideas as a starting point to improve or create new re-tirement plans. During the brainstorming exercise, you were asked to put personal judgments and evaluations aside to allow ideas to flow. Now you can look more closely at the results. If you identified a Life Goal shortfall with your re-tirement plans (page W-5), or if after you re-tire you feel that something is missing, you are probably looking for some new ideas to broaden your plans to satisfy those needs. You have to start somewhere so take a close look at all the suggestions you received and gave, and start with the one that has the most appeal. It may not be prefect, but it is a start.

Figure 10-5

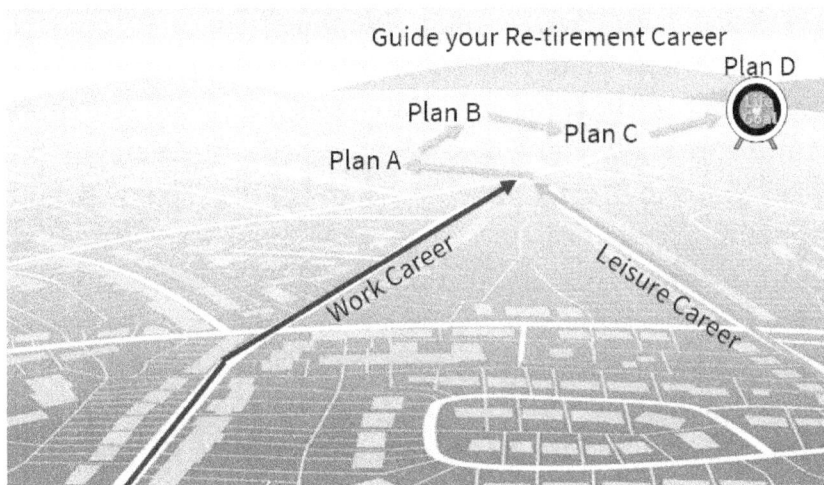

When you re-tire if you are able to pursue activities that satisfy all your needs, you will go directly to your destination. However, things don't always work out that way. As explained earlier, re-tirement is a career that develops and evolves and to understand this process, consider the case of sailing a boat. When you go sailing, you know your destination. What you don't know is the route you will take - that depends on the wind direction.

More than likely you have to tack or zigzag to reach your destination. In this way, you will discover your route, en route. Your re-tirement career will probably be similar. Your objective or destination is to satisfy the items on your Life Goal List but you may have to discover your actual route, en route as you progress through the various activities that ultimately make up your re-tirement career. Here's how it works.

As illustrated in Figure 10-5, start with your re-tirement plan; it could be your original plans or a suggestion from the brainstorming session. We can call this Plan A, and suppose after you re-tire you find that something is missing. To discover what is missing, consult your Life Goal List, select another column, and evaluate each item on your list against your current experience. This will give you an idea of what is missing or how far you are from your Life Goal. Once you identify the items that are missing, brainstorm a new plan - Plan B. You are now basing your brainstorming on your experience with Plan A, and therefore you may come up with something quite new that you might not have thought of before you experienced Plan A. If your next plan is still not perfect, continue the process until eventually you will reach your destination and by finding re-tirement activities that meet your needs and skills. This way you will be guiding your re-tirement career.

To return to my hypothetical example, my Plan A was to spend the winters in a warmer climate, my wife and I were planning to take up tennis, and I thought about finding a part-time job, not necessarily for the money, but for the challenge and stimulation. Suppose after I re-tire my plan did not quite work out. I couldn't find a suitable part-time job and although we enjoy being away in the winter, I sprained my ankle playing tennis, and I am a bit bored. There is something missing from my life. To improve my situation, I look back at my Life Goal List and identified friendships as one thing that was missing so we decided to join a tennis club to take lessons and to meet new people. There, we met a couple who invited us to go hiking. We have never hiked before but decided to join them. It turns out we had a great time with their group on the hike and we spent most weekends hiking. At one point, I volunteered to organize a hiking trip for the group to Europe, and it was a great success. This became my Plan B (a revised Plan A) in Figure 10-5. Based on the success of our Europe trip I developed a website that included an active chat room and I started to organize hiking trips to exotic locations. Now I am earning extra money through an activity I find challenging and stimulating, we are traveling to scout out potential hiking trips and, lo and behold, I have reached my destination and am satisfying all my needs. In fact, I am satisfying more needs now than before I re-tired. In this sense, I discovered my route to re-tirement happiness, en route.

This process can take place before or after you re-tire. Depending on your plans, do your homework, talk to people who are involved in it, read about it, do whatever it takes to find out more about that activity. In the process, and here is the key, you might come up with another and perhaps more realistic or appealing idea that would have never occurred to you had you not started your investigation.

With my hypothetical example, if before I re-tired someone had suggested that I sell exotic hiking trips online when I re-tire, I would have rejected it outright as a ridiculous suggestion. But because I couldn't find a part-time job that was stimulating, was missing friendships, sprained my ankle, and was bored, that led to joining the tennis club, which led to meeting a couple of hikers, and so on. This may take some work on your part and it may take time, but remember, your needs, skills, and interests are unique and you have to get out there to find or create your ideal re-tirement that meets all the conditions on your Life Goal List.

THE DECISION TO RE-TIRE

If you are grappling with the decision to re-tire, here are two additional exercises. Begin by clarifying your reasons for re-tiring. On page W-13, under the Push column, answer the following question, "When I re-tire I am happy to give up…..." Your list should include things you don't like about your work. These can include anything from some of the people you work with, the nature of the task, the hours, location, dress code, politics, and so on. There should be no reference to re-tirement on this list. Just think about the problems or negative aspects of your work. Spend a little time with this and add, as many things as you can to your 'Push' list, no matter how mundane they may seem.

Next, turn to the 'Pull' column. For this exercise you can forget about work and list the things you look forward to when you no longer have to work by answering the following question, "When I re-tire I am looking forward to...." Even if you do not have solid plans for re-tirement, list the things you expect to enjoy in re-tirement. Your list may include things like freedom, sleeping in, travel, more time with my wife/husband/friends, working in my garden, and so on.

Take a hard look at your 'Push' and 'Pull' lists, and compare them. It doesn't matter which list includes more items, the important consideration is to weigh one list against the other. By listing your reasons for leaving or staying at work, it may become clear if you based your decision mainly on push or pull factors. Ideally, you should base the decision to re-tire mainly on pull considerations.

COMPARE WORK AND RE-TIREMENT

You learned how to evaluate your future plans by determining if you could meet each of your needs and skills in re-tirement. You can apply this same process to assist you with the decision to re-tire. Here's how this works. The column on the left side of your Life Goal List is headed Current Life. Ask yourself whether your current work and leisure is meeting each item on your list to your satisfaction. You are not thinking about your future re-tirement, but are concentrating on your current life. Respond to each item with "Y" (yes this item is being met) or "N" (no, it is not being met). You are evaluating a current experience, so there are no question marks in this evaluation.

When this is completed, compare all the data you gathered so far; your needs and skills met through your current work and leisure, your needs and skills you expect to meet when you re-tire, and your 'Push' and 'Pull' lists. With this information if you find work is meeting more of your important needs and skills compared to your pending re-tirement, and that your 'Pull' list is limited, clearly, you are not ready to re-tire. Re-tirement may be a case of going from the frying pan to the fire. It might end up being worse than staying at work (if you have the choice). Having said that, as everyone re-tires eventually, you must change the balance, in favor of your 'pull' considerations. You must get on with the job of finding activities in re-tirement that will be worthwhile and enjoyable.

Alternatively, if the opposite should take place, if your 'pull' considerations are substantive and if it appears that more of your needs and skills will be met in re-tirement than in your current work, there is a strong indication that re-tirement is the preferable route to go. Ideally, you should make this decision independently from financial considerations.

CREATING ACTIVITIES TOGETHER

Say we have two people, Ed and Monica, who want to get involved in a new activity together but have no idea where to start. First Ed brings out his Needs and Skill List. Monica peruses Ed's list and identifies items on his list that she could apply to herself. They write these items on a separate Needs and Skills List. Next, Ed peruses Monica's list and transfers items that could apply to him to the new list. In so doing, they create a combined Needs and Skills List that includes items that apply to both of them. It will probably be shorter than their own lists as all the items on the combined list have to apply to both Ed and Monica. With their combined Needs and Skills List, they can begin to brainstorm suggestions to develop or create an activity that will appeal to them both. The process will be identical to that described earlier, only in this case it involves two people.

SINGLE IN RE-TIREMENT

This issue was addressed in Chapter 8. If you are single before or after you re-tire, and if you feel this can affect your re-tirement happiness, start by adding 'being single' to your Life Goal List (Figure 10-6). Then you can evaluate your plans or try to create new plans based on this additional condition.

Figure 10-6

W-6 LIFE GOAL	PLAN A	PLAN B
Social interaction		
Efficient		
Stimulation		
Responsibility		
Computer skills		
Writing		
Handyman		
Creative		
Holiday		
Relaxation		
Home repairs		
Cooking		
Bicycle		
Exploring		
No hassles		
Being single		

If you become single after you re-tire, and if you feel this is affecting your re-tirement, go back to your Life Goal List, add this element, and reinterpret your current plans based on this new addition. One obvious issue in this context could be friendships. You may want to put extra emphasis on this need when evaluating or creating new re-tirement plans.

CONTINUE THE PROCESS

I encourage you to continue the process. Keep adding items to your Life Goal List by thinking about the six questions listed at the beginning of this chapter, and continue to brainstorm new ideas with your friends, family, and on your own. Finding worthwhile and enjoyable replacements for work is your key to re-tirement happiness, and the workshop is the vehicle that will enable this process. For some it may take time, while for others, it may not be necessary. You have everything to gain and nothing to lose by completing and thinking about the exercises.

LIFE GOAL PLANNNING

WORKSHEETS

RETIREMENT LIFESTYLE READINESS QUIZ

Circle the number between 1 and 7 which best describes how that statement (if applicable) applies to you. There are no right or wrong answers. See page W-3 to calculate your score.

....

A) Attitude Toward Retirement

1. How do you feel about the prospect of retiring

   I dread the thought   1   2   3   4   5   6   7   Looking forward to it/can't wait

2. In general, would you say retirement has a positive or a negative image?

   Very negative   1   2   3   4   5   6   7   Totally positive

3. Would you say that most people associate retirement with growing old?

   Most definitely   1   2   3   4   5   6   7   Absolutely not

B) Spending Time

4. Do you have solid plans for retirement?

   No   1   2   3   4   5   6   7   I know exactly what I want to do

5. Do you have a contingency plan if your first plan does not work out?

   None/haven't thought about it   1   2   3   4   5   6   7   Yes, no problem

6. If you are thinking about working in retirement, would your main reasons be financial or non-financial?

   Strictly financial   1   2   3   4   5   6   7   Strictly non-financial

C) Decision to Retire

7. When you retire, what will your decision be based on?

   No longer enjoying work/job   1   2   3   4   5   6   7   Things I prefer to do in retirement

D) Spousal Relations (If applicable)

8. Have you discussed your retirement plans with your spouse?

   We haven't talked about it   1   2   3   4   5   6   7   Totally aware

9. Is your spouse looking forward to your retirement?

   No   1   2   3   4   5   6   7   Yes

E) Housing

10. Do you plan to move at retirement?

Plan to move   1   2   3   4   5   6   7   Do not plan to move

11. Do you have a contingency plan if your move doesn't work out?

No, haven't thought about it   1   2   3   4   5   6   7   Yes

....
....

F) Friendships

12. Do most of your friends come from work or outside work?

Strictly from work   1   2   3   4   5   6   7   Strictly outside work

13. When you retire will most of your friends still be working?

Most will be working   1   2   3   4   5   6   7   Most will be retired

....

G) Miss From Work

14. What (if anything) do you expect to miss from no longer being involved in your current work?
(Circle or list the items)

Social interaction	Routine
Sense of achievement	Keeping current
Challenges	Sense of community
Contribution	Power
Involvement	Responsibility
Keeping busy	Nothing

Other_____

_____

_____

_____

_____

CALCULATE YOUR RE-TIREMENT LIFESTYLE READINESS SCORE

Total the scores for each section and divide by the number of questions answered in that section. For example, in Section A, if you answered three questions with 6, 4, & 2, your total score is 12 and your average is 12/3 = 4. In Section B, if you answered 2 out of 3 questions (6, 5), your total score is 11 and your average is 11/2 = 5.5. If you scored less than 5 on any section, you have identified an area that requires attention. For section G, the higher the number, the more attention required.

Section	Total Score	Average Score
A) Attitude Toward Re-tirement	_____	_____
B) Spending Time	_____	_____
C) Decision to Retire	_____	_____
D) Spousal Relations	_____	_____
E) Housing	_____	_____
F) Friendships	_____	_____

G) Miss From Work. This is an important element in the transition to retirement and is the basis of the Life Goal Planning Workshop presented in Part 2 of this workbook.

MY RE-TIREMENT PLANS

_____

_____

_____

_____

_____

_____

_____

_____

_____

_____

_____

_____

Life Goal	Plan A	Plan B
_____	_____	_____
_____	_____	_____
_____	_____	_____
_____	_____	_____
_____	_____	_____
_____	_____	_____
_____	_____	_____
_____	_____	_____
_____	_____	_____
_____	_____	_____
_____	_____	_____
_____	_____	_____
_____	_____	_____

Plan C	Plan D	Plan E	Plan F	Plan G
————	————	————	————	————
————	————	————	————	————
————	————	————	————	————
————	————	————	————	————
————	————	————	————	————
————	————	————	————	————
————	————	————	————	————
————	————	————	————	————
————	————	————	————	————
————	————	————	————	————
————	————	————	————	————
————	————	————	————	————
————	————	————	————	————
————	————	————	————	————

W-8

Life Goal	Plan A	Plan B
_____	_____	_____
_____	_____	_____
_____	_____	_____
_____	_____	_____
_____	_____	_____
_____	_____	_____
_____	_____	_____
_____	_____	_____
_____	_____	_____
_____	_____	_____
_____	_____	_____
_____	_____	_____
_____	_____	_____

Plan C	Plan D	Plan E	Plan F	Plan G

_____   _____   _____   _____   _____

_____   _____   _____   _____   _____

_____   _____   _____   _____   _____

_____   _____   _____   _____   _____

_____   _____   _____   _____   _____

_____   _____   _____   _____   _____

_____   _____   _____   _____   _____

_____   _____   _____   _____   _____

_____   _____   _____   _____   _____

_____   _____   _____   _____   _____

_____   _____   _____   _____   _____

_____   _____   _____   _____   _____

_____   _____   _____   _____   _____

_____   _____   _____   _____   _____

W-10

BRAINSTORM SUGGESTIONS RECEIVED

1 _____

_____

2 _____

_____

3 _____

_____

4 _____

_____

5 _____

_____

6 _____

_____

7 _____

_____

8 _____

_____

BRAINSTORM SUGGESTIONS GIVEN
(Brainstorm on your own)

1. _____

_____

2. _____

_____

3. _____

_____

4. _____

_____

5. _____

_____

6. _____

_____

7. _____

_____

8. _____

_____

W-12

LIFE GOAL SHORTFALL

_____

_____

_____

_____

_____

_____

_____

_____

_____

_____

_____

_____

_____

_____

THE DECISION TO RE-TIRE

Push Factors   **Pull Factors**

_____   _____

_____   _____

_____   _____

_____   _____

_____   _____

_____   _____

_____   _____

_____   _____

_____   _____

_____   _____

_____   _____

_____   _____

_____   _____

W-14

UNFULFILLED NEEDS
Important needs or skills that will not be met given my future plans (W-5)

_____

_____

_____

_____

_____

_____

_____

_____

_____

_____

_____

_____

_____

POTENTIAL PLANS

Most appealing plans from my brainstorming session (W-10 and W-11)

1 _____

_____

2 _____

_____

3 _____

_____

4 _____

_____

5 _____

_____

6 _____

_____

7 _____

_____

8 _____

_____

W-16
INCORPORATE LIFE GOAL WITH FINANCIAL PLANNING

The more information you have about how you plan to spend time in re-tirement, the more likely will you or your adviser be able to identify your financial goal and develop a personalized plan based on your future financial needs. To share this information with your wealth adviser, complete pages W-16 to W-17.

Plan A

_____

_____

_____

Financial Implications

_____

_____

_____

Plan B

_____

_____

_____

Financial Implications

_____

_____

_____

Plan C

_____

_____

_____

Financial Implications

_____

_____

Plan D

_____

_____

Financial Implications

_____

_____

Plan E

_____

_____

Financial Implications

_____

_____

SURVEY QUESTIONNAIRE

PART 1: Retirement Plans and Preparation

1. At what age did you retire (semi-retire)?
2. How long have you been retired (semi-retired)?
3. Did you retire by choice or were there factors beyond your control that forced you to retire?
4. Why did you retire when you did?
5. If you could do it over, would you still retire at the same age?
6. As best you can recall, how did you feel about the prospect of retiring just before you actually retired?
7. Did you receive any formal pre-retirement planning assistance before you retired?

   7a. Who provided the pre-retirement planning?

   7b. What did the pre-retirement planning include?
8. Is there any area of retirement planning that you now wish you had given more attention?
9. Looking back, how thorough were you at preparing for retirement?

PART 2: Spending Time In Retirement

10. List the main Leisure (non-work) activities you pursue in retirement.
11. Since retiring, have you ever worked for salary or other compensation?

    11a. Before retiring, did you expect to work for salary or other compensation?

    11b. Is (was) your work after retirement part-time or full-time?

    11c. Is/was your work in retirement related to medicine?

    11d. Was your main reason for working after you retired mostly financial or non-financial?

    11e. What were the main non-financial reasons for working in retirement?

12. Since retiring have you been involved with any unpaid voluntary or charitable activities?

12a. Describe the voluntary or charitable activity.

12b. Were you involved in charitable activities before you retired?

12c. Were the charitable activities you pursued before you retired the same or different from those you pursued in retirement?

PART 3: Housing and Location

13. Did retirement prompt you to move?

13a. Why did you move at or following retirement?

13b. Did you move far enough away that you had to establish new friends?

13c. Any advice for people who are thinking about moving after retirement?

PART 4: Impressions and Advice

14. Everything considered, how would you compare life after retirement to life before retirement?

15. What (if anything) do you miss since from no longer working full-time?

16. In general, how satisfied are you with your retirement?

17. What are the main attractions or benefits of retirement?

18. What (if any) are the main drawbacks or disadvantages of retirement?

19. In general, what advice would you give to other physicians who are contemplating retirement?

PART 5: General

20. Your gender

21. Your present age

22. In general, how would you describe your health?

23. Your present marital status

24. Type of practice

REFERENCES

Introduction

1. Roadburg, Alan, PhD, <u>Aging: Retirement, Work and Leisure</u>, Methuen Publications, Toronto, 1985.

2. Financial Planning Association Web site (www.fpanet.org)

Chapter 1

1. W.I. Thomas and D.S. Thomas. <u>The Child in America: Behavior Problems and Programs</u>. New York: Knopf, 1928, 571-572.

2. Virshup B, Coombs RH, Physicians' Adjustment to Retirement, <u>Western Journal of Medicine</u> 1993 Feb; 158:142-144

3. Scott Highhouse, quoted in The Globe and Mail, June 3, 2011.

Chapter 4

1. Transamerica Center for Retirement Studies, <u>Redefining Retirement: The 'New Retirement Readiness'</u> May 2012

2. Employee Benefit Research Institute and Mathew Greenwald & Associates, <u>Changing Expectations About Retirement,</u> Retirement Confidence Survey, 2012

3. The SunAmerica Retirement Re-Set Study: <u>Redefining Retirement Post Recession</u>, 2011, www.retirementreset.com

4. www.cbc.ca/news/business/story/2012/08/20/cibc-retirement-survey. html

5. Allstate and Matthew Greenwald & Associates, <u>Retirement Reality Check</u>, 2004.

6. Pew Research Center, <u>Working After Retirement: The Gap Between Expectations and Reality</u>, 2006.

Chapter 7

1. Bolles, Richard N., <u>The Three Boxes of Life</u>, Ten Speed Press, Berkeley CA, 1981, 354

2. Doidge, Norman, M.D., <u>The Brain that Changes Itself</u>, Penguin Books, 2007. See also Elkhonon Goldberg, PhD, <u>The Wisdom Paradox</u>, Gotham Books, 2005.

3. American Academy of Anti-Aging Medicine, The World Health Network, <u>Keeping Ageing Brains On Top Form</u>, 2005.

4. Walton, Mark, <u>Boundless Potential: Transform Your Brain, Unleash Your Talents, Reinvent Your Work in Midlife and Beyond</u>, McGraw-Hill, 2012.

NOTES

NOTES

NOTES

www.ingramcontent.com/pod-product-compliance
Lightning Source LLC
Chambersburg PA
CBHW081810200326
41597CB00023B/4208